What others are

"It is an outstanding book for Relapse Prevention. I can see that you have thoroughly implemented the CENAPS Model of Relapse Prevention into the very core of your being. As a result, you have added value to the original concepts. I believe this book is a contribution to the field that you should be proud of."   *Terence Gorski M.A.*

"Her (Linda Free-Gardiner's) sense of humor and gift for simplifying complicated issues makes *Trust the Process* a treasure. After reading this book I feel motivated and yet somehow peaceful, full of joy and hope."

Olive Reed,CRPS, CCDN, CAS

"Most clients respond to these methods with wide-eyed excitement. What a joy to see them get fired-up for recovery."

Jerry Skinner LMSW, LMFT, DCDC

"Trust the Process is an easy-to-read book that tells HOW TO CHANGE, not why to change."

Bobby D

"If you've ever said to yourself, 'Is that all there is to recovery?' this book is for you."

Lisa B.

"What a joy to read a recovery book with hope instead of hopelessness. Ms. Free-Gardiner's sense of humor is also a gift that shows throughout the book."

Sue Day

i

Trust the Process

How to Enhance Recovery and Prevent Relapse

Linda Free-Gardiner

First Edition

Newjoy Press
Ventura California USA

Trust the Process
How to Enhance Recovery and Prevent Relapse
by
Linda Free-Gardiner

Published by:
Newjoy Press
Post Office Box 3437
Ventura, California 93006 USA

Copyright © 1996 by Linda Free-Gardiner
First Printing 1996
Printed in the United States of America

Library of Congress Data

Free-Gardiner, Linda
Trust the Process: How to Enhance Recovery and Prevent Relapse
by Linda Free-Gardiner. --First Edition.
Includes bibliographic references and an index
1. Relapse Prevention - Counselor Guidebook
2. Drug Abuse - Relapse Prevention Treatment
3. Alcoholism - Relapse Prevention Treatment
4. Chemical Dependency - Relapse Prevention Treatment

616.8   1996   95-78914
ISBN 1-879899-03-5   Soft-cover $15.95

Dedication

To my lover, best friend and partner
Tom

and

To Connie Weston and Kathy Bortko who laughed in the face of eternity and taught me the meaning of courage.

Charitable Contributions

In the spirit of returning what has been graciously given, the author will contribute a portion of all of her profits from the sale of this book to recovery based charities and causes.

Table of Contents

Illustrations

Foreword
by
Terence T. Gorski M.A.

Author of
Staying Sober: A Guide to Relapse Prevention

You are in for a treat! *Trust the Process: How to Enhance Recovery and Prevent Relapse* lives up to its name. This book offers hope for recovering people at any level in their growth - newcomer, oldtimer or the chronic relapser. Emphasizing personal development, Linda Free-Gardiner points the way to sustained, happy recovery.

Relapse is a serious problem in the Chemical Dependency and Behavioral Health Field. Nearly two out of every three chemically dependent persons who attempt sobriety will relapse. Most of the relapses occur within the first six month of attempting recovery. The problem is even more serious among those who also suffer from personality and mental disorders.

Obviously, there is a desperate need for practical applications of Relapse Prevention Therapy to help people who are unable to recover with traditional chemical dependency and psychotherapy methods. The techniques needed must be effective, practical and easy to learn. *Trust the Process* gives you the needed techniques.

Linda Free-Gardiner, a Licensed Chemical Dependency Counselor, was one of the first in the country to certify as a Relapse Prevention Specialist. She is a founder and past-President of the National Association of Relapse Prevention Specialists and led the field in outcome research on the effectiveness of Relapse Prevention Therapy.

I've watched Linda's career with great interest over the past years. Her primary love and interest is in the treatment of relapse-prone persons. In clinical practice, her dedication is obvious. The work she has done in simplifying and applying the basic relapse prevention principles is impressive.

Trust the Process is a unique application of the CENAPS model of treatment. The book integrates many practical tools, techiques and ideas about relapse prevention therapy. It is well written, easy to read and easy to understand. The diagrams and creative applications of ideas are singular. Linda has drawn upon her own experience and that of other Relapse Prevention Therapists to make this book a comprehensive guide to recovery enhancement. It is a "must read" for any therapist or recovering person with serious interest in adapting relapse prevention methods to the real world of everyday problems.

About the Author

Linda Free-Gardiner has been in private practice in Houston Texas for nine years, specializing in addiction relapse prevention. Her sense of humor and personal recovery experiences flavor her work and add a realistic dimension to her writing.

She has presented hundreds of workshops on relapse prevention.

She was one of the first Licensed Chemical Dependency Counselors to respond to the need for relapse prevention. She certified as a Relapse Prevention Specialist and has made relapse prevention her mission in life.

Linda has been the clinical director of two intensive outpatient programs for chemical dependency treatment.

She has written many articles about recovery enhancement and relapse prevention. Her goal is that through this book she will reach thousands of therapists and individuals who will benefit from the techniques and the encouragement contained in its pages.

Acknowledgments

Learning about addiction has been an exciting adventure. Many were there along the way to offer their wisdom. Among these were Terry Gorski, H. Lee Slavin, Tammy Bell and John Cook.

Hundreds of patients and friends graciously offered their experience, strength and hope. They provided the foundation for Trust the Process.

Stephen Covey is a silent partner whose concept of a personal mission statement propelled my endeavor. One day I will thank him in person.

Grateful thanks to my team of reader/reviewers: Bonnie Zannini, Ellen Joe, Emily Blondeau, Lisa Beck and Olive Reed.

Other cheerleaders who helped me acquire the courage to write: Rachel and Tom Gardiner, Eileen Bennick, Sue Day, Evelyn Canady and the Sunday Morning Gang.

To each of you a heartfelt, "Thank you."

Disclaimer

This book is designed to provide information in regard to the subject matter covered. It is sold with the understanding that neither the publisher nor the author are engaged in rendering therapy or other professional services through this book.

Every effort has been made to make this book as complete and accurate as possible. However, there may be mistakes both typographical and in content. Therefore, this text should only be used as a general guide and not as the ultimate source of relapse prevention information.

The purpose of this book is to educate and entertain. The author and Newjoy Press shall have neither liability nor responsibility to any person or entity with respect to any loss or damage caused, or alleged to be caused, directly or indirectly by the information contained in this book.

If you do not wish to be bound by the above, you may return this book to the publisher for a full refund.

CHAPTER 1

INTRODUCTION

*"When love and skill work together,
expect a masterpiece."*   John Ruskin

This is not a book. It is a process. At the
end, if you work the exercises, you will have a
different perspective on what your recovery can
mean and what relapse truly is. You will have a
renewed vigor for life if your experience is like
that of hundreds of others who have used this
method. I call the method *Trust the Process*
because that concept is a vital part of making the
Recovery Enhancement Program (REP) work.

As you read, work through the exercises
and practice the tools, you will have many
unexpected feelings. You may say to yourself, "I
must be doing this wrong." Don't worry.
Everyone thinks that from time to time. The truth
is, it's very difficult to sabotage the process if you
keep going. When you start hearing your self-talk
about your reservations, say aloud the words,
"Trust the Process".

Many people make sticky-notes of this

saying and paste them in critical places, like on a mirror, in the car, or on the refrigerator . . . places they'll see frequently. This reminds them that all is going just as it is supposed to go.

Who can benefit from the Recovery Enhancement Program?

Anyone who has recurring patterns of dysfunction in their lives can benefit from this process. And you need not know exactly what the pattern is in the beginning. The program helps you identify underlying, unconscious patterns keeping you from your goals.

It is not necessary to have returned to the use of chemicals to be a good candidate. In fact, it works very efficiently with individuals who have been sober for six months, five years, fifteen years. You see, drinking or drugging is but a symptom of our disease. *Where have I heard that before?* It is the recurring patterns of dysfunction that are eating our lunch. REP works directly with those recurring patterns. Some very effective candidates are those with five years of abstinence having trouble coping with life's problems.

The word "relapse" has such a negative connotation that by using it in conjunction with Recovery Enhancement, some people make the sign of the cross and run. Don't worry, it's not contagious. The truth is, the way to enhance one's recovery is to find a means to stay out of Dry Relapse. Chances are if you never experienced Dry Relapse, you would have no need to read this book. By finding the fastest, most efficient way out of Dry Relapse, you allow more time for the fruits of the program. Thus, recovery is enhanced.

I am licensed to treat chemical dependency, meaning alcoholism and drug addiction. Therefore, most of the focus of *Trust the Process* is on chemical dependency. No therapy has a guarantee. Not one. But, I have been told by many who are trained to treat other disorders such as codependency, eating disorders, and sexual addiction, that they find REP's techniques very helpful and effective for such maladies.

Note, I make no assurances of any kind that REP works with these disorders, but if you are a therapist trained to deal with such problems and you find these techniques blend with your methods, you are not alone.

This book is derived from a series of workshops taught to therapists across the United States. Few seats are left at these workshops because there is a tremendous hunger and thirst on the part of therapists and counselors to help patients prevent relapse. In fact, a 1994 Gallup survey done by the National Association of Alcohol and Drug Abuse Counselors asked its 19,000 members what educational topic they wanted most. A startling 59% said they wanted education on Relapse Counseling.

What does it mean to Trust the Process?

A process is a continued forward motion; a series of actions. Imagine a row of dominoes standing on end. For some reason the first one is tipped over. One falls and strikes the next one in the row and then the next one falls and this actions continues until they all are down. That's a process. Unless someone interferes with the process of the dominos falling, the end is inevitable.

That's the same idea here. If you are an appropriate candidate, participate to the best of your ability and don't purposely interfere with the process of Recovery Enhancement, it will significantly move you along the road of your recovery.

Why Trust the Process?

Trust doesn't come easily. You all need evidence to support it. An in-house outcome study provides some of that evidence. It was conducted within my private practice, where the REP has been operating and developing for the past eight years.

An outcome study takes into account all patients of a certain type or profile and asks "How did they come out at the end of your treatment?" It can examine a variety of things but in this case the primary concern was abstinence rates. Relapse prone alcoholics who repeat standard treatment for chemical dependency following a wet relapse episode average a recovery rate of approximately 16% nationwide. Not very good odds, is it? In fact, many of the counselors and therapists who seek training from me say that they believe the recovery rate to be much lower than this. In other words this group of folks rarely find significant periods of abstinence.

The outcome study on the methods used in my practice showed an 83% recovery rate on a population that averaged 3.4 wet relapses prior to this treatment. From 16% to 83%!

I don't claim to be an incredible therapist. I'm not. What I have to offer you is a process that works. And it works with amazing results.

Another piece of evidence that this process works is found in the comments of past clients, counselors and therapists. Here is some feedback.

"When I started this therapy I'd been sober for seven years and was a counselor myself. I didn't want to drink, but I was so miserable I wanted to die. Most of this program is so straight forward that I can't believe I never heard it before. Somehow this process opened my eyes, sharpened my hearing, and saved my life. It also helped me get out of the way of my husband's recovery," Terry P., sober now thirteen years.

"I think you will find Relapse Prevention Therapy to be a common sense approach to escaping the cycle of addiction. The process clearly guides you through very intense work that gets to the bottom of what's killing you; and it

just plain makes sense," Jerry Skinner, Licensed Master Social Worker, Licensed Marriage and Family Therapist and Licensed Chemical Dependency Counselor.

What qualifies me to write such a book?

Fair question. I am a Certified Relapse Prevention Specialist, a Licensed Chemical Dependency Counselor, a Certified Clinical Supervisor and Master Addiction Counselor. My practice focuses primarily on dry or wet relapse prone alcoholics and addicts. More details of my credentials are on the author's page.

Primarily the theoretical basis for the Recovery Enhancement Program is Terence Gorski's powerful CENAPS Model of Relapse Prevention Therapy. He is widely accepted as the pioneer and a leader in the field of relapse prevention. I have had the privilege of learning my craft directly from Terry and to participate as faculty in his certification school.

The Recovery Enhancement Program utilizes CENAPS theories, as well as Rational Emotive Therapy and Behavioral Modification techniques as the basis for its highly effective program. Any clinical practitioners who find REP interesting, I strongly urge to explore Gorski's books, (listed in the bibliography), and his Certification for

Relapse Prevention School. Both literally changed my life.

I have an absolute passion for addiction relapse prevention. Fascinated with it for years, I have been searching for and developing new ways to help those who long for healthy, happy recovery. I believed from the beginning that abstinence does not equal recovery. There had to be some clear way to assist others in achieving true recovery. The Recovery Enhancement Program developed from this passion.

My search, however, has been more than a professional mission, it's been a very personal experience for me. Because, "Hi! I'm Linda. I'm an alcoholic and an addict," who relapsed twelve years ago. That experience and my own quest to be happy, joyous and free has taken me on this search for knowledge of relapse prevention information, techniques and methods.

While I learned from many pioneers of the relapse prevention movement, I also learned by listening and respecting hundreds of recovering people who taught invaluable lessons of recovery enhancement and relapse prevention.

How to use Trust the Process.
This book is written with three purposes in mind.

First, an individual who is working alone on their recovery can utilize it. There are certain exercises wherein having a partner is helpful but you can do them alone. If you get stuck on one of these exercises I would encourage you to network for a like-minded soul to assist. You can also seek professional help, but advise the therapist exactly what your purpose is in seeing them.

Second, a group of individuals can benefit greatly by using this as a study guide. The accompanying workbook will be a bonus and may dramatically increase your works' effectiveness. This method I suspect will be much more beneficial than by one's self. By bonding together and sharing the experience, you can also keep focused, motivated and supported. Besides it's fun.

Third, clinical practitioners may increase their success and personal satisfaction practicing these methods. This work was originally conceived with a clinical perspective but I quickly realized that I teach clinicians in exactly the same way I teach clients. It was a perfect blend. Experience is a terrific teacher.

The best way for a therapist to learn this model is to practice it using their own life experiences. You become the client. That's how I learned it. If you learn by doing too, you're in for a treat and more than one AHA! Not only is it an effective way to learn this method, but by doing the work myself, I was freed from lifelong bondage.

My goals for this book are simple.

1. Layout the Recovery Enhancement Program in a way that enables clinicians and recovering people to put its principles to work immediately. As you read along, it is my hope that you will find something vital for your recovery in each chapter.

2. Motivate readers to action. To provide you with the plan is not enough. If REP is laid out well, it inherently provides the motivation to act, to practice utilizing the tools, and to grow.

3. Empower creative thinking. As the spirit grows, reaches further, and expands our horizons, the creative power within us is released. I believe it is this power that fuels the recovery engine.

4. **Have fun**. Life is trying. Personally, I find learning experiences much more beneficial if I can laugh along the way. Life is much too serious to take it that way.

5. **Secret Goal.** I have a very special goal in mind and I ain't telling. Well, not until near the end. **STOP!** I know somebody just decided to flip to the end and check it out. You'll spoil your own

experience if you do. Remember, this isn't a book, it's a process.

Where do I begin?

Many have said, "Is this all there is to recovery? I'm not much happier than before!" To them I suggest they read and work this book. Now, I'm not suggesting that if you couldn't play the piano before this book, you will afterwards! I am suggesting that you may well experience a startling awakening. You may find the true source of what it is that trips you up time and again. If so, you'll develop an effective plan to deal with it.

I can hear you saying, "I already know what trips me up and I'm still doing it. This won't help."

Well, here comes the first suggestion I'll make. Set aside for now your belief that you already know what the problem is that keeps you locked into your troubles. You may find that your absolute belief that Problem X is your source of difficulty, is the very reason you can't see the true Problem A. Perhaps your focusing on Problem X keeps you too dazzled to see Problem A, let alone deal with it. At any rate, please try to set aside the belief that you have already figured out your entire life, neatly boxed the components and put them away. Why would you want to read this if

11

you had? This is the point to begin.

However, if you find you can't put this belief out to pasture for a few months, don't worry. You can find your path anyway. The beauty of the Recovery Enhancement Program is that it helps you see right through your deeply ingrained denial systems.

A search for truth.

In 1982 a desperate woman downed the last 25 or so of her Valium pills. In a sick ceremony she said, "good-bye" to her worthless life. She didn't want to wake up again. She left no note. There was no way out of her hell. She was trapped. Years of drinking and prescription drug addiction robbed her of dignity, spirit and hope.

Her plan was thwarted when her husband came home unexpectedly, and with his heart aching and full of self condemnation, he rushed her to the emergency room just in time.

After two days she knew she had to do something drastic. In an odd way the suicide attempt provided motivation adequate to search out a better way of living. At the suggestion of a therapist, she was hospitalized for inpatient treatment for addiction. Being the hero of the family, she quickly adapted and decided to do whatever it took to, "make A's in the course."

She did just that. She became very active in recovery and went to lots of 12-step meetings. She worked her steps. She was as honest as she knew how to be. She found a sponsor. . .the works. A flush of new life force infused her steps. She felt connected and had a real purpose as goals for her life were forming.

Everything sailed along just fine until five months later. For the first time her husband left on a business trip. It didn't occur to her that it was a dangerous time for her sobriety. After all, she was doing great. And then she drank.

A week later she was in another treatment center, her head spinning. How did this happen? She felt she had been struck drunk. It's only supposed to happen if you don't do what you're supposed to do. They said she wouldn't relapse if she read the Big Book, went to meetings, got a sponsor, worked her steps. Something was desperately wrong. Her confusion was amplified by detoxing again. Was this worth it? Was it all a lie? Maybe it couldn't be done at all. She wondered "Am I the 'constitutionally incapable of being honest' one they talk about at meetings? I'm worthless. I can't even get this sure thing right." The pain was excruciating.

Her sponsor and recovery group said, "You just didn't work a good first step." That confused her all the more. She could have sworn she had.

They said, "The answer is in the Big Book." But at that time the Big Book of Alcoholics Anonymous was not even understandable for her. How could she get answers from it? She had the feeling her friends were asking her to put a bandaid on a surgical wound. She was hemorrhaging emotionally but she followed their directions. If they'd said she needed to stand on her head for a week, she would have.

When the fog cleared she began to make a detailed analysis of what had happened. She began to see markers of trouble present before the relapse, but not noticed. For instance, her big toe had been aching for days before she drank. She realized this was because she was clenching it, a frequent response to unacknowledged anger. Since she had never learned to deal with anger she channeled it into a physical symptom.

Using this symptom as a clear indicator of trouble in the future, she knew that if her toe ached she had to take immediate action to prevent another relapse. She finally felt some sense of power in her own life again. She vowed relapse would not sneak up on her again.

"She" is me. It was from this background that I tenaciously sought truths about the nature of relapse, its symptoms, and methods to deal with it. I'll never forget the first time I heard Terry Gorski talk about relapse warning signs and equated them to my self-discovered sign of the aching toe. It was as if someone had been reading my diary. I felt elated that at last someone understood and could describe my experience in a way that made sense. A language for relapse. What a terrific step forward.

I have never stopped my quest.

For those of you who have experienced a wet relapse, you are not alone.

CHAPTER 2

FOUNDATION FACTS

"Opportunity is missed by most people because it is dressed in overalls and looks like work."
                                                    Thomas Edison

There's more than one right way.

No two people are alike, yet recovery programs have almost universally treated everyone the same. The Recovery Enhancement Program suggests we recognize the perfect individuality of people. Instead of deciding that everyone needs to follow exactly the same plans to find their pathway, REP suggests there are a number of unique methods to that end.

Think of a carpenter. They wear extremely well designed tool belts which enable them to have lots of powerful, effective tools within easy reach. With practice and skill, they know just where each one is, what it's best used for and how to get the job done.

That's REP at a glance. The recovering person becomes a carpenter. They are given a well designed set of tools, which they can put into their belts at easy reach. They are provided with a structure that encourages them to practice using

16

these tools and developing skills. They learn just where each tool is, when to apply it, what it's generally best used for and how to get the job done.

Recovery Enhancement suggests the clinician become a guide in the acquisition of these tools. This implies two things. First, clinicians must know what the tools are and second, they must know the best use for each. The most effective method for learning how to utilize this program is to practice using the tools on your own life experiences. Whether you have an addiction or not, if you apply these methods in your life, chances are you will see their power.

The Recovery Enhancement Program is a growing, evolving method. When you begin to practice it, you will probably discover a new tool or application that substantially improves it. Great! Write me. I'll be very excited to hear from you and will recognize your contribution. You see, I do not believe that any one person has THE SOLUTION. I do believe that if we work together, allowing for the creative energy of each person to expand, we can trigger powerful synergistic ideas. By empowering others to contribute, tremendous progress will be made toward designing the best programs of recovery opportunities.

Addiction to substances is a disease.
If your insides danced when you read that

sentence, you have work to do. We have more studies and clinical evidence to support the truth of that sentence than you can imagine. In fact, there's been more studies done on alcoholism than on any other illness, bar none. More than cancer, heart disease, HIV, you name it. Yet, we as a society continue to insist that addiction is behavioral or, worse yet, a moral issue.

It is imperative for long-term, fulfilling recovery that we understand, accept and believe this simple truth, addiction is a disease. There is a film by Dr. David Ohlms, distributed by GWC, Inc., called simply, *The Disease of Alcoholism*. This film is a mainstay in any treatment I'm associated with. It is a powerful film of a physician explaining in plain English the disease of addiction. It is a terrific means of shame reduction for both those who have chemical dependency and their families. I recommend it to everyone.

Having a disease means I need not be ashamed of it. I wouldn't be ashamed if I had heart disease, or diabetes. There was a time when our society attached a stigma to the disease of epilepsy. Many of you can remember a time when we called seizures, "having a fit". There was an innuendo that the seizure victim somehow "brought this on." Since that time much has

I am especially aware of the parallel because I am also epileptic. When I first discovered this, I felt intensely embarrassed and ashamed, and denied it to be a problem. Just like the alcoholic, I looked for other obscure reasons for the episode.

However, once I was reassured that this was a medical fact, not a moral failure, and realized that the rest of the world treated epilepsy as such, I could accept it, take the medicine and live symptom free. So it is with alcoholism and addiction. Once we recognize it is a medical fact our shame is reduced, we can stop looking for obscure reasons to explain away our "episodes", take the medicine (in this case not drugs but 12-step programs or spiritual programs), and live symptom free.

Minimize self destruction to enhance recovery
Recovery is an amazing process. You grow; you are happier than before; you have life problems; you consider possible answers and choose the one for you; you work through the problems; you learn their lessons; you try new principles; you grow, etc. The circle goes on and on.

The recovery process is a perfect combination of growth, happiness, other opportunities to grow and learn new methods of handling problems. The struggles you have while looking for new solutions to problems are not bad. They may be part of the lesson you are supposed to be learning.

When the recovery circle happens to you as described above, your struggles are beneficial. You will eventually realize their purpose and benefit. When you understand, you will internalize better ways of thinking and new principles.

A subtle difference in the recovery process circle takes you on the path to misery. It happens like this: you grow; you are happier than before; you are confronted with life problems; you refuse to look to others for possible answers; you either blunder your way through the problems or deny they exist; you don't work through them; you don't learn their lessons; you decide others are to blame; you don't grow, you are coasting,etc. You end up with no growth, no solutions and increased pain.

Did you notice where the two processes began to differ? At the point between being confronted with life's problems and looking to others for answers, something happens. It may sound as if the answer at the point of divergence is simple . . . look to others for possible answers . . . it is not. Something within the addictive personality will not allow this to happen. That "something" is critical. It is Dry Relapse.

In *Trust the Process* you will focus on recognizing, managing and minimizing the potential for Dry Relapse.

You don't have to break your abstinence to be in the relapse process.
Well, there's a bit of heresy.

People who are dry as Texas tumbleweed can be miserable as the devil. Relapse is a process. So is recovery.

Many, many people with five years abstinence sit down in my office because they're miserable. They are the lucky ones who can overcome the shame of the idea that they have done something wrong in their recovery. It's a myth that you'll never fail in recovery if you work the program well. (More information on this in Chapter 4.)

Recovering persons can learn from the process of relapse and prevent it from ruling our lives. Relapse is not right or wrong. It is a fact. When you take the right-wrong, good-evil out of the picture, it begins to clear up substantially.

Recovery is a constant journey.
We are always moving, either moving up or down. Picture the downward flow of an escalator. Your work in recovery is to go up on that down escalator. There's the process in a nutshell. It's

work, constant work. You can't coast. If you stop moving ahead on a down escalator you're going backwards. You're *never standing still.* You may like the illusion that you coast in recovery. It's only an illusion. If you are not going forward, then you are going backward on that escalator and you are in the relapse process. Those are the only two options. You are either in the recovery process or in the relapse process.

The Recovery Process

You grow
You are happier than before
You are presented with life problems
You look to others and a Higher Power for answers
You consider possible answers and choose one.
You resolve the problem
You learn new lessons
You try out new principles . . .

You grow
You are happier than before.
You are presented with other life problems . . .

Interrupted Recovery Process

You grow
You are happier than before
You are presented with life problems
You refuse to look to others or a higher power for answers.
You either blunder your way through or deny the problem exists.
You can't work through them.
You don't learn their lesson
You decide you or others are to blame.

You don't grow
You are coasting, believing you are okay.
You are presented with similar life problems.
You struggle but can't resolve them.
You don't learn their lesson.
You believe you are being cheated in your recovery. You are often angry.
You decide others are to blame

You are stuck! Around and around you go.

You can do the 12-Step Program right and still relapse.

More heresy. This is a very threatening truth to recovering people. There is a widely held belief that if you do it "right", you'll get sober and stay sober. There's great comfort in that idea. It means you can relax. But it's a lie.

Lots of things can trigger the beginning of the dry relapse process. Some of them have nothing to do with 12-step programs at all. A medical illness can trigger it. Going to the dentist can trigger it, if it's then necessary for you to take certain addictive medications for pain. Unfortunately, our bodies don't recognize the difference between legitimate medical need for pain killers and "Party Time!!"

I'm not saying that if you're in recovery you should never take any pain medications. There are instances that may require the use of such drugs (i.e., surgery) or a serious accident. What I *am* saying is that many recovering people do not realize the danger they are in when they use these medicines and therefore, don't protect themselves adequately.

This is one of several examples of someone who may be doing their "program" quite well, but relapse anyway.

You can't relapse until you've made it into recovery.

Relapse is about the return to an active disease process following a period of recovery from that disease process. One very important fact . . . you can't relapse in any disease until you've been in recovery from it. This is the truth in any illness. If someone has not yet gotten into the recovery process they cannot have a relapse. If that abstinent-but-not-in-recovery individual uses or drinks again, they are merely continuing their disease. They must prove to themselves that they can't drink or drug like normal people. The fact that they may put together a little abstinence time is misleading.

Abstinence does not equal recovery

This is an important concept. If it takes someone several periods of abstinence and "dabbling in the 12-step program" in order to actually begin their recovery, they may tell themselves they "relapsed" six times already. However, they were never truly in recovery so those six times had nothing to do with relapse, they were part of their disease.

So what happens when that person finally is wholeheartedly in recovery, making a solid effort, trying everything they can to stay sober and then they use or drink? They tell themselves, "This is my seventh relapse. You see, I knew I couldn't do this thing even with my best shot. I give up!"

Can you see the danger of perpetuating this misinformation? It was really their first relapse. But they have already condemned and heaped shame upon themselves. Others, even their support group, may have reinforced their shame and blame.

Having a relapse doesn't mean the person, "Has not suffered enough . . .", to get sober.

I cringe everytime I hear someone repeat this sentiment. It may be true for a small percentage, those who have not yet made it to recovery and are only dabbling in sobriety. These people may be trying for someone else's benefit but haven't decided to do it for themselves. But it's an awful label for those who are truly relapse-prone, meaning they are trying hard but just can't seem to stay sober. In the first place, suggesting someone has not suffered enough is a judgment call. Who are we to judge?

Consider this, you got abstinent from

chemicals four years ago. Excellent! Since then you realized that nicotine was not good for you, that you were probably addicted to it as well, that it is killing you as surely as your other addictive chemicals.

You decide one fine Tuesday that tomorrow is the first day of your nicotine recovery. You go along fine for eight days (although you have thrown up, pulled your hair out, shouted obscenities at the minister, gone to 800 meetings and killed every plant in your house). Then on day nine you smoke again. Does this mean you haven't suffered enough?

Think about it.

The Recovery Enhancement Program does not replace 12-step programs.

From my clinical observations and all the data available, the 12-step programs are the most successful programs for recovery. REP is not meant to detract from or compete in any way with AA, NA, PDAP, OA, etc. While the 12-step programs are the most successful method, they are definitely not successful for everyone who tries them. REP is designed to work together with 12-step programs. Twelve Step and REP . . . a dynamite team.

DEFINITIONS

Recovery is the process of becoming more functional while abstinent. Increasing function is demonstrated by acquiring principles such as, honesty, maturity, acceptance, assertiveness, and humility.

Enhanced Recovery is a lifestyle that is so reinforcing that giving it up for use of a chemical becomes impossible.

Dry Relapse is the process of becoming increasingly dysfunctional while abstinent. Dry relapse always precedes a wet relapse.

Notice it is not an event. I would wager that a great many more of us suffer from these dry relapses than ever imagined. In fact, many live their entire "recoveries" in a state of dry relapse.

There are many people with multiple years of sobriety who are miserable and fall into this category. It is likely that most of us in recovery have had significant periods we can identify as dry relapse. I certainly can. Since dry relapse always precedes a wet one, if you become good at identifying a dry relapse you may prevent the wet one from happening.

Wet Relapse is the actual use of chemicals by a formerly abstinent individual. This is what is traditionally called a relapse. I urge you to

31

separate this from a dry relapse. This distinction is very important.

Process is continued forward motion; a series of actions. Imagine a row of dominoes standing on end. First one falls, then the next, then the next, until the last one finally goes. The significant fact about a process is that one thing leads to another in a systematic way. Hang on to the domino image, it's important later.

Primary Treatment is the traditional Minnesota Model of chemical dependency treatment focused on 12-step philosophy, education of the addiction process and penetration of the denial systems. Almost everyone who gets professional treatment for addiction is placed in some form of Primary Treatment.

Relapse Warning Signs or Relapse Dominos are self-defeating behaviors that are symptoms of a dry and/or wet relapse which become progressively more intense, eventually resulting in a mental or physical breakdown and may or may not include a breach of abstinence. These signs are predictable and allow intervention. There are many Relapse Dominos on the path to a drink or a drug.

Gorski's CENAPS Model of Relapse Prevention Therapy is a therapy designed specifically for the relapse-prone alcoholic or addict. It uses "relapse warning signs" as a way to find deeply ingrained patterns and their sources. It empowers the integration of thoughts, feelings and actions and reduces the need for self-defeating behaviors which lead to relapse.

Rational Emotive Therapy developed by Albert Ellis suggests that by straightening out their thinking, people can straighten out their actions. The basic idea is that irrational thoughts lead to exaggerated feelings and self-defeating actions. Thoughts lead to feelings which lead to actions.

> ## *A SECRET GOAL is a terrible thing to waste*

CHAPTER 3

CLIMBING RECOVERY HILL

"One doesn't discover new lands without consenting to lose sight of the shore for a very long time."　　　　　　　Andre Gide

Recovery Hill is difficult to climb. You begin the climb because you are miserable. It's seldom for any other reason. Yes, outside forces may be on your back, but it's your internal misery associated with those outside forces that really moves you along. Later, of course, you will climb for other, more positive reasons.

There are many lessons to be learned along the climb. Each one is necessary before you can learn the next, more difficult lesson. One major problem you will encounter in your efforts to climb the Recovery Hill is the desire to jump ahead.

Perhaps it's grandiosity. Whatever the reason, you decide you are not required to complete your recovery work in any kind of order. You begin attempting tasks that are much further up the hill before you complete the necessary ones in between.

The difficulty with trying the climb like this lies in the fact that the tasks in between were

34

necessary to build the skills critical to accomplishing the later tasks.

Here's an example. Some of the early tasks on Recovery Hill include things like "*Learning Level One Stress Management Skills.*" Since drinking and drugging was your major coping skill, it makes sense to better develop new ones before you subject yourself to major stressors.

However, in your rush up Recovery Hill you skipped the learning level task. Then you decide to go to work on your childhood abuse issues. Encouraging this random issues approach is a very common mistake made by well meaning therapists and friends.

It is not difficult to see that childhood abuse issues are among the most stressful and painful problems any person, recovering or not, ever works at resolving. If a newly recovering person has not developed *Level One Stress Management Skills* (not to mention Level Two or Three), how on earth can they cope with doing such emotional work without drinking or drugging? It's a pretty tall order.

Take a look at the drawing of Recovery Hill. Find the location of the task called *Exploration of Childhood Issues.* It's about ninth from the top. Way up there! Count how many tasks are supposed to be completed before that one? At least a Gazillion.

I am not saying that a person should never deal with these issues in early sobriety. Sometimes it's a necessity. If the person gets into recovery, honestly tries the program and then relapses, indeed other issues (sometimes childhood abuse) may be in the way. But for the most part, working on childhood abuse issues is a late recovery task.

Of course, if a person is having flashbacks or powerful images of a past abuse episode, it must be dealt with to some degree. But be aware, these issues are difficult for anybody. Get professional help. Whether you have financial resources or not, get help. It's available from many sources if you keep looking. You must figure out how "not to drink or use today" on a consistent, effective basis before you can possibly tackle your other tough emotional issues. And don't try it without a net!

The single, most effective thing you can do to prevent relapse is to enjoy the trip up Recovery Hill. Hard to do? Yes. Do-able? Yes, though pleasure will be intermittent. Nevertheless, keep climbing that hill.

Starting from the bottom, read the items on Recovery Hill. Which steps have you completed?

Which task are you currently working on?

It is reassuring to have a delineation of the tasks of successful recovery. Many times in recovery, you may feel as if you are drifting, unsure of your next step. The Recovery Hill paradigm will clearly show you what comes next. A clear path is not only a profound relief, it can prevent you from sliding back.

RECOVERY HILL

CONTINUE GROWING

Return their gifts to society
Manages Life Transitions
Level 4 stress mgmt.
Increase Intimacy Skills
Works Step 11
Discovers Personal Creativity
Management of Childhood Issues
Works Step 10
Exploration of Childhood Issues
Works Step 9
Level 3 Stress Management Skills
Begins balancing other life areas with program
Works Step 8 ·
Releases other compulsive Behaviors
Begins working Step 12
Accepts personal responsibilities
Works Step 5, 6 & 7
Learns Deferred Gratification
Internal Dysfunction subsides
Self-regulates recovery program
Values begin changing
Works Step 4
Level 2 stress management skills
Decrease in shame about disease
Work Step 3
Education and acceptance of addictive disease
Stabilization of motivating "problems"
Begins to hope
Works Step 2
Learns level 1 management skills
Obsession to use /drink fades
Obtains and regularly communicates with a 12- step sponsor
Withdrawal completed
Works Step 1
Begins consistant 12-step attendance
Finds out can't do it alone
Tries recovery alone
Finally accepts necessity of total abstinence
Falls again
Attempts to control use of chemical
Normal means don't work
Tries to solve addiction "problems" by normal means

FORCE OF GRAVITY

MISERY

38

Impediments to Climbing Recovery Hill

Inability to Think in Abstracts

Because of the neurological damage done during alcohol and drug addiction, newly recovering people have an inability to do abstract thinking. They are very concrete. That means that to try to conceptualize something that is abstract (meaning you can not feel, see or touch it) is an impossibility. They simply can not do it. Most newly recovering people can only think in concrete terms.

For instance, if you tell the recovering person, "You'll have freedom from the obsession of alcohol if you don't drink," (freedom and obsession are abstracts) they may nod their head (they don't want you to think they are "defective") but believe me, they probably don't understand it. But if it is expressed, "If you get sober, you won't have to stay at the bar every day until it closes," then they can understand. This is concrete.

If you are communicating with someone who is struggling with abstract thinking, tell them what you want to communicate by a story. Express your abstract concept, but then follow it with, "That's like when . . . " Then you'll be understood. The other person won't become frustrated and self-condemning.

If you are the person who is having trouble understanding the meaning of what others are telling you but you are embarassed to tell them so, here's a simple solution. Ask for examples. The speaker will probably have to express the abstract idea in a concrete way if they give you an example. If one example isn't enough, ask for more.

Also, it has been my observation that while this phenomenon is most prevalent in the newly abstinent, it also seems to be episodic for those who have been abstinent for longer periods. Many of the people with whom I've worked in REP who were multiple years abstinent in "The Program", were still having reccuring problems with the inability to abstract.

You are not alone if you find you have difficulty with abstract thinking. It seems to be an almost universal problem among recovering people. This is normal for you, me and all addicted persons.

The good news is, for most people, the difficulty will go away. All you need to do is wait. There is no need to push yourself or others who are in this state. In fact, "pushing" may slow down the process.

Not recognizing the inability to abstract is a mistake made over and over. In fact, it is systematically carried out. One of the very first things a newly recovering person is given is a Big Book of Alcoholics Anonymous (called the Big Book). Newcomers are told, "All the answers are in this book."

It is true that many powerful solutions are in the Big Book. However, it is one of the most abstract books around. So the newcomer reads it, scratches their head and goes back to the person who gave them the book saying, "I don't understand it."

They are then told, "Just keep reading it, son, the answers are there."

The newcomer looks at the book and back in the mirror and says to his image, "You see, I knew I couldn't do this. I can't even understand the book. How could I possibly follow its directions."

Please do not misunderstand me. I believe the Big Book is invaluable. Everyone becoming abstinent should read it. I'm saying that when you suggest the Big Book as *the* cure for a person's disease and then they find they can't understand it *at the time*, you have unwittingly set the person up for failure. The best approach concerning the Big Book is to go slow. Wait until they are ready.

Try providing the newly abstinent with a written list of instructions, such as "Go to at least one meeting a day, eat three balanced meals and two snacks, call a sponsor or recovering person every day, don't drink or drug, tell yourself you can drink or drug tomorrow if you still can't stand this problem." All concrete, understandable usable tips. In about a month or so the fog will begin to lift and their ability to abstract will begin to return. Be patient

There is one explicit book a newly recovering person can comprehend. I recommend it as a basic text on addiction. It is *Learning to Live Again,* by Merlene Miller, Terry Gorski, and David Miller. I have everyone in my program, whether they are newly sober or long-term abstinent, read this. I read it at three years and again at five years and learned information that both comforted and enlightened me.

Post Acute Withdrawal

Post Acute Withdrawal, also known as long-term withdrawal, is a group of symptoms called a syndrome, occuring after the end of acute withdrawal. This syndrome can make normal daily living very difficult. The symptoms include difficulty thinking clearly, memory impairment, emotions that are extreme, trouble in sleeping, stress reactions, and even clumsiness. The symptoms appear in episodes that tend to come and go. They last for varying lengths of time.

The good news is that this syndrome is normal for recovering people. Just plan on having trouble with this from time to time. Most people do not have all these symptoms at once - thank goodness.

Some people have only mild symptoms of Post Acute Withdrawal and so it impairs their life minimally. Others have more intense problems, for longer periods and with more extreme symptoms. It is suspected by Certified Relapse Prevention Specialists that those who have greater difficulty with this syndrome are in the category of relapse-prone. This certainly has been validated in my practice with this population.

What's the connection? Just imagine, you're six weeks sober, you wake up in the morning after having your third restless night's sleep, your emotions are all over the map, you can't remember things that you normally don't have trouble remembering, and to top it off you keep bumping into things. Charming, huh?

Then you go to work. You're trying to prove to the boss the time they gave you off to "dry out" was well invested. Except you can only remember two of the three assignments the supervisor gave you yesterday.

You start obsessing with the thought, "What's wrong with me? Maybe I just can't hack it in the real world. Maybe I have some kind of permanent brain damage."

The more you think this way, the more depressed and full of self-hate you become. Then your supervisor asks if you've completed that third assignment. You react defensively and decide you're being persecuted. You storm off.

After work, on the way home, as the steam, anxiety and fear is billowing from your brain, you stop for a coke at the corner store. You walk in. The first thing you see is a round barrel full of iced beer. You tell yourself this is a message from God. Glug, glug.

The next day you are shaking your head saying, "How did that happen?" That's what life is like for some people who are suffering from severe Post Acute Withdrawal Syndrome.

The good news is that Post Acute Withdrawal is manageable. There is an enlightening chapter about this phenomenon and methods for dealing with it in the book *Staying Sober*.

CHAPTER 4

UNDERSTANDING DRY AND
WET RELAPSE

*"As scarce as truth is, the supply has always
been in excess of the demand."*
                                          Josh Billings

Only 45 years ago the recovering community
was a mere handful of people with a strange new
idea of talking to other drunks about not drinking.
Up until that time only two percent of those
attempting sobriety achieved it. That translates to
a 98% rate of return to drinking and/or drugging.

Alcoholics Anonymous World Services, Inc.
reports an estimated 1,127,000 current members
in the United States and 1,790.528 members
world wide as of January 1, 1995

With all these folks getting involved in 12-step
groups you would think the abstinence rate would
be high. Think again. Wet Relapse is actually
more common than abstinence!

According to Gorski, the national average of
those maintaining first time abstinence for at least
one year is 33%, so there are 67% who use or
drink again. Of those 67% it appears half will get

back into abstinence and put together significant clean time. That's the good news. But it still leaves about 33% who never put together sustained long-term abstinence. Ask yourself, who is kidding who if it is said abstinence is the norm for people trying to get sober?

I do not want to give you the idea I believe treatment "fails" in 67% of the cases. The Cal Data Study conducted by the University of Chicago for the State of California clearly proves treatment works.

When the study examined employment rates, recidivism (return to criminal behavior) and illnesses of treated persons they saw dramatic improvements. In fact, this study shows that for every $1 spent on treatment $7 is saved. Money is saved on incarceration, medical bills, loss of productivity and many other items. While many people may not achieve abstinence right away, they may have begun to climb toward that goal.

Look again at the beginning of the Recovery Hill. It addresses the job of figuring out that drink/drug is "my problem," and "I need help to stop". It's not unusual for a person to use their substance a few times while "proving" those things to themselves.

What is this phenomenon we call relapse? First, separate out wet and dry relapse. For reference's sake here are the definitions listed in Chapter 2.

Dry Relapse is the process of becoming increasingly dysfunctional while abstinent.

Wet Relapse is the actual use of chemicals by a formerly recovering individual. In the case of someone who is recovering from a compulsive behavior, it would be the acting out of that specific behavior, i.e., a sex addict having an illicit sexual encounter, or an abstinent alcoholic taking a drink of alcohol or using drugs.

Wet relapse follows a dry relapse. It is not the other way around. Unfortunately, many people have the idea that wet relapse happens from, "out of the blue." People have wet relapses because they act their way into a dry relapse. This is the Relapse Process. The concept, "If I'm not using or drinking then I'm okay," is bologna.

To prevent a wet relapse, getting good at

identifying and stopping the dry relapse is critical.

Taken from this perspective, the dry relapse is far more insidious than a wet one. Yet there is little if any emphasis in the 12-Step programs on the phenomenon of dry relapse.

The most extraordinary event of my personal recovery came in the midst of a 12-Step meeting where the topic had turned to dry relapse. The leader was incensed. He shouted that there was no such thing as a dry relapse. He was so sure there was no such thing that he threw a chair just to prove it. That was pretty graphic proof to me that people don't like the idea of a dry relapse.

> People have wet relapses because they act themselves into a dry relapse.

There seems to be a kind of paranoia in 12-Step circles about dry and wet relapses. If you have attended meetings where someone is discussing the subject you may have sensed an electricity in the air. Sometimes you can almost taste the fear.

I want to debunk some ideas about relapse:
- ☐ Relapse is not contagious
- ☐ Relapse is not the enemy

- Relapse does not strike, "Out of the blue."
- Neither does relapse wear a sign that says, "Hey, I'm coming! Better take immediate action."

What have you believed in the past about relapse? Take a few minutes and a piece of paper. Complete the following sentence, *I believe relapse is . . . .*

Start writing. Keep writing until you have eight or more answers.

Next write the sentence, *I believe relapse is caused by . . .* and repeat the process.

Last try this sentence, *I believe the best my recovery can be is . . .,* and give eight more answers. Go ahead, I'll wait.

Back already? Were you surprised by what you wrote, or not?

Remember in the introduction I asked you to suspend your beliefs? Try it here. If you hang on to all your old ideas about relapse, you probably won't have room for new ones. Now that you know what your old concepts are on the subject of relapse, let them go while you read this book. Put them in your "Spirit Vault".

A Spirit Vault is a container into which you "turn over" problems or situations requiring assistance from a higher power (described more in

Chapter 11). Take the paper on which you wrote the answers, fold it up and put it in the vault for now. If you want your old ideas back at the end of the book, they're right there waiting.

Sliding into relapse

The Dry Relapse process is moving backward down the Recovery Hill - from functional recovery into dry relapse. Resulting in wet relapse and/or emotional breakdown. Locate your current status on thie hill, then make it two steps worse. That's where you are most likely to be. Almost everyone has a misconception about where they currently are on the hill.

A dry relapse begins when you are faced with a life problem. Facing a life problem isn't unusual in itself but this time you are unsuccessful in dealing with this particular problem because in order to solve it you would have to go against a personal internal rule called a survival rule.

These are rules you all have and may or may not be aware of. Some are rules you established years ago. They kept you safe then, providing a way to survive an extremely threatening or traumatic time. But now these survival rules interfere with your ability to face problems directly.

For example, your sponsor has not returned your call for three days. If you were going to solve this problem you would have to:

1. Notice that you are angry.
2. Try to verify with your sponsor what has happened.
3. Confront the sponsor appropriately.
4. If not satisfied, accept it or change sponsors.

Simple, right? Well, suppose your survival rule says, "I must never show anger or else they'll leave me." In this case, the survival rule may have been formed in childhood when you believed your anger caused your parent to leave you. You may not be aware this is a rule for you, but you operate by it, nonetheless.

This internal rule comes up against your life problem. Because your internal survival rule assures you that something awful will happen to you if you show anger, instead of paying attention to the problem and dealing with it, you say, "This is not a problem. There's nothing wrong."

But, of course, there *is* something wrong and the problem doesn't go away. You become more and more angry with your sponsor. You stew in the thought that he/she, "Should know you were angry, after all, and should apologize, by God." You get a juicy resentment going. Voila, the recipe for the beginning of a dry relapse process. Solving this life problem requires you to go against your survival rule.

Can you see how your deeply ingrained belief, "I can't show anger or else they'll leave me," prevents you from dealing effectively with an average, everyday problem for a recovering person?

This may sound like a minor life problem. How does getting angry with your sponsor constitute the beginning of a dry relapse? Remember the definition of a process is continued forward motion, a series of actions, the domino effect. The first domino has to fall in order for the second one to fall. The second has to fall before the third, etc.

The Domino Effect of Life Problems

Domino 1. My sponsor does not call me.

Domino 2. I'm hurt and angry but pretend it doesn't matter. My survival rule, "I can't get angry or they will leave me," prevents me from dealing with my problem appropriately.

Domino 3. I decide she didn't call because . . . I select a self-centered reason such as, "She didn't call because I'm not worth her time." This is a self-centered reason because it implies I think her life should revolve around me and my actions.

Domino 4. I stew in anger and develop a resentment.

Domino 5. Because I feel resentment, I avoid calling my sponsor.

Domino 6. Because I avoid calling my sponsor, I don't talk about my feelings

Domino 7. Because I don't talk about my feelings, I get confused and can't think clearly.

Domino 8. Because I'm confused, I don't do my job well.

Domino 9. Because I'm not doing my job well, I start worrying about being fired.

Domino 10. Because I'm worried about being fired, I am short with my husband.

Domino 11. Because I'm short with my husband, he snaps at me.

Domino 12. Because he snapped at me, I want to stay away from home.

Domino 13. I want to stay away from home but I can't go to AA because my sponsor is there, so I think about going to my old hangout where people love me for who I really am.

Domino 14. Because I go to my old hangout, I am faced with a high risk situation with drugs or booze readily available in a place where I've used before.

Domino 15. Because I'm angry, alone and think this recovery thing isn't working anyway, I decide that drinking or drugging was a better way of life after all.

Domino 16. I drink or use drugs or perhaps act out another compulsive behavior.

The dominoes are down.

The cycle continues.

The domino effect is a process, a logical sequence of events. One thing smoothly leads to the next. It starts out very small. The problem is quite minor. Because that survival rule cannot be challenged, the tumble down the relapse slide begins.

Notice how the process becomes more and more intense. Each domino provides increasingly severe life consequences. By the time all the dominos have fallen you've become so miserable that drinking or drugging actually seems like a good idea.

From this example of dry to wet relapse, notice three things:
1. Something prevents you from handling life problems appropriately.
2. Often you are not aware of what is happening.
3. If you could somehow stop this process early, you could prevent the later consequences and misery.

Learning the information in this chapter may be intimidating for many people. Some may notice a growing unease, confusion or downright fear. This is good news. It's good because it means the process is working. It is a sign that you are questioning your stance on issues and making room for new ideas.

Your uncomfortable feelings do not mean a wet relapse is imminent. Feel the feelings but push ahead with your Recovery Enhancement work. The path will become clear to you as you walk it. This is a place to practice trusting the process.

CHAPTER 5

PRIMARY TREATMENT

"The trouble with the rat race is that even if you win, you're still a rat."   Lily Tomlin

Recovery is the process of becoming functional while abstinent. Note the word *process*. One thing has to happen before the second thing can happen and both have to occur before the third thing can happen. Having trouble with advanced recovery issues may well be rooted in lack of a good foundation. If you missed some piece critical to the development of your program, then you need to go back and fill in the missing piece.

Not everyone attempting to get sober needs Primary Treatment. Some people are able to walk into 12-Step groups and soar. They utilize the 12-Step program and do just fine. Others, for reasons we do not always understand, are able to get sober with no assistance at all or by less mainstream approaches.

However, those who manage to attain sobriety without at least the structure of a 12-Step program are in a very low percentage. It is not surprising that almost everyone tries the, "I don't need any help" method of getting sober. But very few actually do find abstinence that way.

Primary Treatment is the professional help provided to those who are making their first attempt at getting sober or who have relapsed. Until recently this was the only treatment style available. In the past few years, the CENAPS method for relapse-prone individuals has become prominent.

Notwithstanding, Primary Treatment is still the foundation upon which recovery is built. It is generally provided in a setting called Intensive Outpatient which means after work treatment three to four nights a week for three hours per night. It generally lasts 6-8 weeks. The tasks and goals of Primary Treatment must be met in order for your recovery to be on a sound basis.

In my estimation Primary Treatment often provides a much needed head start for getting a good recovery program started. There are a great many tasks to be done in order to move from a life that is centered around addiction to a life centered around healthy principles and the exclusion of the use of chemicals.

Skipping Primary Treatment can be equated with trying to go to high school before you go to kindergarten. Some could probably manage the advanced classes, but many more will have an extremely difficult time by skipping kindergarten and all the classes in between.

Major goals of Primary Treatment

☐ **Introduction to 12-step philosophy** is learning about what the 12 steps are, how they work, and how a support group can best be used.

☐ **Connection to 12-step group** is achieved by regular attendance at a home group. A home group is a place where you attend meetings daily for 90 days and very frequently thereafter and where you begin to feel relatively comfortable.

☐ **Obtaining a sponsor** is the act of getting a guide within your home group. You ask someone who demonstrates what you consider to be strong recovery, with at least 2 years sobriety. Preferably their addictions are similar to yours. The sponsor's job is to act as a helper, teaching you how to utilize the 12-Steps in your daily life. The sponsor is also a model. They show you and tell you how they reached and now maintain their sobriety.

☐ **Completion of written first step** is an assignment involving writing. In most programs it is a series of questions designed to help you look at your entire problem, to see it as it really is, not as you imagine it to be.

☐ **Education about the addiction process** is a class teaching the nature of addiction, helping you to understand the process experienced and the difficulties which will continue into sobriety.

☐ **Recognition of the need for total abstinence** means absorbing the truth that there is no alternative chemical that will be okay to use . . . period. None, nada. No way.

☐ **Penetration of the denial system** involves lowering of the defenses that prevent you from seeing the truth concerning a very wide spectrum of realities affecting your life.

☐ **Establishment of communication within the family system** means the opening of honest, open discussions laying out the truth and preparing to practice a life and relationship based on truth and respect.

☐ **Acceptance of personal responsibility** happens when you stop blaming others for what has happened to you. The recognition of your own accountability opens many doors.

☐ **Establishment of a support network** consists of adding a number of recovering individuals to your circle of friends. Choose people with whom you feel safe when discussing your problems. This group of friends often provide you with a new, sober social group.

☐ **Establishment of your recovery program as the first priority in your life** consists of actively making recovery work the most important task of your life, for now. Any conflicts that arise, demanding your time and attention, for the immediate future, must give way in favor of the recovery program. Recovery work must come before spouse, children, work, fun, church, everything . . . for now. The *for now* part of this statement is often overlooked and leads to big problems with this concept. Recovering people tend to be all or nothing thinkers. Therefore, they think, "If I have to make this my number one priority now, then I have to do it for the rest of my life and I know I can't do that!" They can thus provide themselves with a perfect rationalization for not doing recovery work at all.

Let's go back to the fact that addiction is a disease. It is primary, chronic, progressive, and left untreated, it is fatal. Just like cancer. Just like diabetes. If you were diagnosed with cancer and the doctor said you needed chemotherapy, nothing, absolutely nothing, would keep you from those treatments. Not your spouse, not your job, not your yard, not your boat, not a baseball game - nothing. Your life hangs in the balance.

Chemical dependency requires the same kind of dedication to treatment in the beginning phases. Your 12-step meetings are your chemotherapy. So is getting a sponsor and communicating, and working the steps with them. You don't have to like it. People don't like chemotherapy either, but they do it. Think how fortunate you are. Treatment for your disease won't make you vomit or lose your hair or any of the other sufferings cancer patients must endure. But make no mistake. If you do not make treatment your number one priority, you will suffer a fate every bit as serious and deadly as that cancer patient.

Recovery Enhancement Program tasks not attained in Primary Treatment.

☐ **Preparation and presentation of a Relapse Intervention Plan** is an exercise available in the REP Workbook. The purpose of the exercise is to help the recovering person set up a system to intervene should a dry or wet relapse begin. It describes to a significant other what behaviors they might see if the recovering person starts sliding toward a dry relapse.

The next step gives specific instructions to the significant other about how to intervene to help the recovering person recognize the trouble and get back on track. The recovering person reads the completed document to their significant other. It's a powerful experience.

☐ **Completion of Daily Inventories** is another exercise in the REP Workbook. One of its functions is to provide a specific list of the daily regimen required to maintain and encourage growth in recovery. Another function of the exercise is to offer a chance to look at neurological symptoms plagueing most recovering people and to examine methods for dealing with those symptoms. The exercise ends with a gratitude list.

☐ **Acceptance of the disease of addiction** differs from the education on the subject which primary treatment programs offer. People learn in their heads what addiction is, but never buy in their hearts that they have a disease. They cling to their socially ingrained view that addiction is a bad habit, or a moral failure, or worse, sin. The step from knowledge to acceptance is often the difference between self-forgiveness and self-loathing.

There are some major flaws with Primary Treatment Programs. Whether you are experiencing treatment for the first time or have relapsed 15 times, Primary Treatment is the only treatment available for chemical dependency in most places. This is a serious problem. I ask you, if Primary Treatment did not work the first 14 times, why would it work the 15th?

Statistically, the chances are Primary Treatment will only work 16% of the time for the relapse-prone person. These are appalling odds.

So, what else could a person do? A Relapse Prevention Treatment program run by a Certified Relapse Prevention Specialist is designed specifically for the needs of a relapse-prone alcoholic or addict. I have practiced this model for years and have seen it's effectiveness first hand.

Here's a consumer tip. If you call almost any treatment center in the U.S. and ask, "Do you have the Gorski Model of Relapse Prevention Treatment?" They will probably answer, "Yes!" Mind you, they may not have a clue what it is but the marketing folks are sure they have it.

Some treatment providers confuse the generic term with the specific treatment modality, thinking, "We all do relapse prevention treatment."

Try asking the question this way, "Do you have the CENAPS Model of Relapse Prevention Treatment and, if so, who is the Certified Relapse Prevention Specialist on your staff?" If they haven't got a CRPS on the staff then I guarantee, they aren't doing adequate Relapse Prevention Treatment.

If you are Trusting the Process you are increasing in faith

CHAPTER 6

FUNDAMENTAL CONCEPTS OF THE RECOVERY ENHANCEMENT PROGRAM

"We are so accustomed to wearing a disguise before others that eventually we are unable to recognize ourselves."   La Rochefoucauld

Have you ever come upon one of those crazy pictures you see in the mall or at some galleries where the entire canvas is taken up by a repetitive and meaningless design? Then someone swears to you that if you just look at the picture from the right angle, you'll see something entirely different within that design.

You may have to use different strategies like not focusing your eyes as you gaze at it or by half closing them. By applying these techniques, some people can see through that "covering design" to the art beneath. Inevitably, the moment they do they say, "AHA!"

This is the essence of the Recovery Enhancement Program. Lives are filled with repetitive and *seemingly* meaningless patterns. REP teaches you the techniques and exercises that allow you to see through the patterns to the true beauty beneath. Then, at the moment you find your way through the patterns you say, "AHA!!"

We have discussed the dry and wet relapse process and the beginning tasks of the Recovery Hill accomplished through Primary Treatment. This chapter focuses on the critical junction where your progress up the Recovery Hill begins to slip down the Dry Relapse Slide. Sometimes all the way down to a Wet Relapse.

It may seem as if everything is going fine one month and the next you're miserable enough to act out, doing things you wouldn't have considered last month. What triggers this change?

This bridge from recovery to relapse is a process, too. One event has to precede another. For identification sake I call this the Triggering Bridge. (See drawing on page 87.)

The drawing illustrates how the climb up Recovery Hill is cut off by the Triggering Bridge, followed by a Dry Relapse and, often, a wet one.

I hear you now, saying, "But that's not what happened to me. I haven't had a wet relapse." Many people in recovery work have found themselves in a Dry Relapse and somehow managed to cut it off before they actually used the

68

chemical or engaged in behavior from which they are abstinent.

The drawing on page 71 illustrates this cycle of Interrupted Recovery. In *Staying Sober*, Gorski describes this as, "partial recovery." I believe most people in recovery get stuck in this cycle at least once and sometimes repeatedly.

The cycle begins when you begin the trudge up Recovery Hill. You do what it takes. You work hard. Then you experience a Triggering Bridge. You may be unaware it is happening. The experience kicks off the slip into a Dry Relapse. You become progressively more uncomfortable. Slowly your problems are compounded and you get closer and closer to a Wet Relapse.

However, you have enough recovery skills to recognize that you are in big trouble somewhere along the Dry Relapse Slide. You say to yourself, "I think I'd better go back to my basic program. I'm going to work hard at it until things get smoothed out." This is an Interrupted Recovery.

So you start up Recovery Hill again. You work like the devil. You make progress. But guess what? You didn't resolve the source of the trigger in the first place, which means you will encounter it again. Bang, another Triggering Bridge happens and you slip down the Dry Relapse Slide again.

Around and around and around you go.

Because you never figure out the source of the Triggering Bridge, it happens again and again. Many of us have been through this cycle repeatedly.

Let's look at the components of that Triggering Bridge. (See page 87) The parts of the Triggering Bridge are:

1. A pattern of similar life problems
2. A set of Survival Rules
3. A Soul Wound.
4. Missing Universal Principles

Triggering Bridge

RECOVERY HILL

AROUND AND AROUND WE GO

AROUND AND AROUND WE GO

DRY

RELAPSE

SLIDE

Recognition
of Danger

RETURN TO BASICS

FOCUS ON RECOVERY.

YOUR LIFE
DEPENDS
ON IT!

There are some new words in the preceding section. How about definitions?

Soul Wounds

A Soul Wound is a very painful, generally long-term problem that is a chronic source of misery. I think of the Soul Wound as an open, painful gash that sears right to the soul. It may be abuse, it could be a parent leaving or dying, it could be adult trauma, it could be any number of serious issues not yet resolved.

Now, this Soul Wound could be healed. But recovering people are often blind to what is needed to heal the wound or they lack the skills or willingness to resolve it. Think of the Soul Wound as having a hole of a specific shape in the center. It could be a circle or a star or a triangle. Choose a specific shape. By nature, recovering people are constantly seeking to fill this hole and heal the wound.

Have you had this sense of searching? You try drugs, you try alcohol, you try other people, shopping, gambling, you name it. On an unconscious level there is an intense urge to find the missing piece to make you whole.

Survival Rules

A Survival Rule is a strategy each person

develops to prevent re-injuring their Soul Wound. We all have a natural instinct to protect whatever part of us that is hurting. If you've ever had a broken wrist, arm, foot, leg, you notice that appendage becomes the center of your world. You go to great lengths to keep others from touching it. God forbid anyone should step on the injured foot or jostle the injured arm. You go around in semi-terror waiting for someone to hurt you again.

Well, imagine how you would protect a searing pain reaching right into your soul. It's far worse than any broken bone or torn ligament!

Just as you develop physical strategies to protect a broken limb from being jostled, you develop emotional strategies to keep the Soul Wound from being touched. In fact, you've done it so long that it has become second nature. You don't even notice you are protecting something, or that you even have these strategies.

In this process these are called Survival Rules. And all recovering people obey them as if their lives depend on it. Being highly resourceful people, you customize your set of Survival Rules. You design them to protect a very specific Soul Wound.

Survival Rules generally take the shape of thoughts that begin with, "I must, I can't or I should" messages. You believe in your heart that if you obey these generally irrational rules, you will prevent your painful Soul Wound from being jostled and hurt further.

You act out your life around these irrational rules. They begin to dictate what you do or don't do, where you go, who you talk to . . . even your choice of occupation. It's amazing.

Say one of your Survival Rules is, "I can't trust others or else they'll leave me just like my mother did." You probably developed this rule to protect the deep Soul Wound you experienced when your mother left you as a child. It is a pain you never resolved. You acquired this Survival Rule to prevent anyone from abandoning you again.

Chances are you are not even aware you allow this rule to dominate your life. Perhaps, you have operated out of this rule for so long you don't even realize you have it.

Unfortunately, the end result of keeping the rule is exactly what you seek to prevent. Since you trust no one, they all leave you anyway. Who wants to be around someone who doesn't trust them? But since this thought process happens on a subconscious level, you believe you were right in the beginning . . . people can't be trusted.

As a matter of fact, you search the world looking for people who will help you prove to yourself that your Survival Rules are true. If we find enough support for this irrational belief system, you never have to change it.

You probably think you are already aware of your personal Survival Rules. Indeed, you may be aware of some of them. But very few people have an adequate handle on what their Survival Rules are. Often people can't identify their Soul Wound, so they don't know the source of their rules.

Universal Principles

Addiction leaves many deficits in its wake. When you started sobriety work, you began to realize this. For instance, there is a gulf between the social skills of an average thirty year old American and the social skills of a newly recovering thirty year old person. Many learned to socialize in addictive settings, but not outside them. Some recovering persons were already into addiction as teenagers when critical skills should have been learned. Many never acquired assertiveness skills. Many were unable to set boundaries. Set them? Heck, most of us didn't even know what they were!

The 12-Steps of AA are designed to teach a set of Universal Principles. The idea is that your addiction short-changed you in this area and that only through adopting and practicing these principles can you effect life-long change.

Of course, the founders of AA in the Akron group did not get this idea out of thin air. It has been taught for centuries. It is Biblical. Early philosophers taught the notion of self-improvement through principle-based living.

Stephen Covey's enormously popular book and workshops entitled *Seven Habits of Highly Effective People* espouses the same idea in an intriguing and powerful way. (A list of some Universal Principles is on page 79.)

Let's assume you and I have deficits in the Universal Principle department. Deficits in Universal Principles are a large part of the Triggering Bridge.

A helpful way of measuring progress in recovery, or lack thereof, is by the acquisition of these principles. It's a bit tricky measuring for yourself, though. It appears that people gain these principles slowly, a bit at a time. For example, you might have had 20% honesty five years ago and have 60% honesty now.

When discussing honesty, I don't mean only cash-register honesty. I am also referring to honesty about feelings, desires, goals - the really *important* stuff. (The Workbook provides an exercise to assess your progress in becoming honest).

You remember the discussion under the

definition of Soul Wounds? It described a searching we undertake to fill a void, a specific *hole* associated within that Soul Wound. This hole, I believe, is the link between the Soul Wound and Universal Principles. I picture these principles in specific shapes; circles, triangles, stars. Likewise the *specific hole* we want to fill is envisioned as circles, triangles, stars.

It is a perfect, God-made fit. I have a *specific hole* for which one or more Universal Principles are an exact fit. Universal Principles are the balm needed to heal the Soul Wound.

Picture this. You have a Soul Wound and a set of Survival Rules designed to protect that Soul Wound. You are constantly searching for some way to heal the wound. Unconsciously, you know this remedy is a specific shape, though you don't know which shape. You try all kinds of shapes (drinking, drugging, shopping, people) but they never fit, they're not the remedy. So you keep looking.

> *Universal Principles are the remedies needed to heal Soul Wounds*

At the same time you are on the hunt for a

healing remedy, you have developed your Survival Rules to protect that poor wound of yours. Unfortunately, it is these very Survival Rules that prevent you from finding your remedy. Survival Rules interfere with your acquisition of the Universal Principles needed to heal your specific Soul Wound. So the hunt continues.

Survival Rules
prevent you from finding the remedy
for your
Soul Wound

Universal Principles

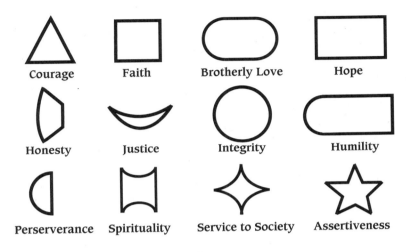

Courage	Faith	Brotherly Love	Hope
Honesty	Justice	Integrity	Humility
Perserverance	Spirituality	Service to Society	Assertiveness

SURVIVAL RULES

SOUL WOUND

"I MUST, I CAN'T"

The Soul Wound could be made whole
by applying a specific Universal Principle.
However, our Survival Rule keeps us
from applying that Principle.

Pattern of Life Problems

Working with relapse-prone people has made me very curious about why people can deal with certain life problems but other life problems cause people to stumble. I have noticed there is a similarity in the type of problems that trip up a specific person. It seems they are confronted over and over with similar, seemingly unsolvable life problems. They shake their heads and say, "Not again!" But indeed, that same old type of problem is back.

Many great works of philosophy, religion, and recovery suggest life problems have a purpose. Could it be the specific life problems causing us repeated trouble have something to teach us? Perhaps these problems will continue until we learn whatever it is we need to know.

Let's go back to the concept of searching for something to fill the hole in your Soul Wound. Perhaps the lesson of these particular life problems is somehow connected to the filling of our Soul Wound's hole? It seems logical since we are constantly searching and constantly being confronted with the same situations. Maybe there's a reason!

REP suggests that in order to solve these similar life problems you must learn to apply the very Universal Principle eluding you. This turns out to be the same Universal Principle needed as the healing remedy for your Soul Wound.

The reason this series of similar life problems occurs is to give you one more opportunity to heal that Soul Wound. You see, if you can acquire that Universal Principle, you can begin healing both the Soul Wound and your recurring life problems.

What a coup!

Next Month's
Life Problem

Next Week's
Life Problem

This Week's
Life Problem

SOUL WOUND

Pattern of Life Problems

We have a consistent pattern of
similar life "unsolved" problems.
We similtaneously encourage
and repel these difficulties.
The inability to solve them triggers slide into relapse.

How the Soul Wound Triggers Dry & Wet Relapse

Universal Principle
would begin healing
the Soul Wound
(Courage)

"I must"

"I can't"

**SOUL
WOUND**

Pattern of
Life Problems
*(People put me
down. I overwork)*

Survival Rules
*(I must work harder
to prove I'm worthy
or else they'll leave me.)*

SOUL WOUND
(Childhood neglect)

My "friend" cuts me down in front of 12-step group.

I need to apply principle of courage, tell her the behavior was
unacceptable and tolerate the feelings that come up when I do that.

I can't do it because I believe I'm unworthy anyway and
probably deserved being treated like that because
I haven't been working hard enough.

I start working extra hours at my job.

I don't have time for the people at my 12-step group.

I get angry because I'm working hard
and they don't notice.

I perceive somebody else puts me down.

I think I'm more miserable sober than drunk.

I stop going to meetings.

I become severly depressed.

I begin binge eating to cope with the feelings.

I decide to go to the bar where
other lazy, low-lifes
like me hang out.

I drink.

DRY RELAPSE

**WET
RELAPSE**

 MISERY

Example of a Triggering Bridge

To illustrate how this theory works go back to the example in Chapter Three. Refer to the chart on page 55, *The Domino Effect of Life Problems.*

To recap, the chart describes a person who develops a resentment against her sponsor because the sponsor didn't call her. The Soul Wound in this illustration was a parent leaving the person when she was a child. The child made the conclusion that the parent left her because of her anger. The Soul Wound grew because of the issues around her father's abandonment of her.

As a result, she began a life-long habit of smothering her anger. In fact, she has made such a good job of it that she will swear she never gets angry at all. Of course, every time she felt something that might have approached anger she squashed it. Quite possibly with the use of chemicals.

In recovery, though, she doesn't have chemicals or acting out to deaden the anger. It's here and it's big and it won't be ignored. The bigger it gets, the more threatened she feels and the harder she tries to enforce her Survival Rule.

In our example, the Universal Principle in question is honesty. This principle is in direct conflict with her survival rules. Her survival rule engenders thoughts that she can't be honest with her sponsor because of her belief she cannot afford to tell her sponsor she is angry. She has a bone deep fear her anger could "cause" her sponsor to leave her just as her anger "caused" her father to desert her. Subconsciously, she believes another abandonment will be more pain than she can survive.

Notice this is not just any Universal Principle her Survival Rules have come up against. It is THE Universal Principle that might help heal her Soul Wound. Possibly the person in our example has many life problems that she could solve if she were to learn and apply the principle of honesty.

Wham! Her Survival Rule puts her in direct conflict with the very Universal Principle that might heal her Soul Wound. Imagine the fireworks! Her conflict with THE Universal Principle starts her down a relapse slide.

Thus, for this person, getting honest (acquiring THE Universal Principle) about her feelings of anger with her sponsor and afterwards realizing that her sponsor doesn't leave her, could be the tool she can use to begin healing her painful wound concerning abandonment by her parent.

What's more, that type of Life Problem may cease to recur. After all, once she learns the lesson what would be the point? She would no longer need that life problem.

Is that all there is to it?

From the examples included here, one could get the idea that by the acquisition of one particular principle, your life would magically heal. That, of course, is not reality. However, this is one place where trusting the process comes into play. For the present time, there is only one particular principle it is time for you to learn. You need to find out the reason these specific problems are presenting themselves.

It is quite possible, indeed likely, later you will need to acquire another principle. Then a whole different set of problems designed to teach you *that* principle will occur. You need to accumulate many principles on the road to recovery, but they seem to appear in perfect order. You only need to concentrate on the one directly in front of you.

Now you know what to do. Want to know how?

You now have the foundation, the theory and the basics of the Recovery Enhancement Program. Remember how a process works? You must build the foundation before you construct a mansion. For the rest of this book you will learn, step by step, how to move past stumbling blocks to continue upward on Recovery Hill. Fasten your seat belts!

THE TRIGGERING BRIDGE

△ Apply Univ. Principle

HILL

Survival Rules

Life Problem

△ SOUL WOUND

RECOVERY

DRY RELAPSE

CHAPTER 7

TELLING THE HISTORY

"Fear is that little darkroom where negatives are developed."   Michael Pritchard

Your work begins at the beginning. You can't pick up the threads in the middle of a ball and expect to be able to sort it all out. Yes, I'm sure you've told your story before. I can hear you groaning now. I moaned, too, when I did this work for myself. But at the end you will see how vital it was to the PROCESS. This is where you begin a strategy to see beneath the *cover design* to the art of who you are.

Two consistent ways people short circuit this program is they:
1. Skip the directions and try to do the exercise with no information or guessed-at information.
2. Completely skip exercises they believe "aren't necessary" for them.

If you choose one or both of these routes, you will not get the full benefit from the program. Each suggestion is very specific and designed to complete the process. Therefore, I suggest you do yourself a favor and read the directions first and complete every exercise.

I add this little warning because I am notorious for thinking I don't need directions or that I am just way too advanced to need this silly little exercise. WRONG!

The most efficient way to make use of this chapter is to combine it with exercises six and seven in the workbook.

Purpose of telling the history.
The stories of recovering persons are basic to recovery. Though you undoubtedly have told your history before, this time it will be laid out a little differently in a prescribed format. The format is designed to widen the view of your personal history. Equally important, the history begins a process of examining patterns.

The process begins by taking a wide angle view of your life's past events through a pair of sharp glasses. Later you will be taking ever tighter looks, eventually through a microscope, at the events which shaped your life. The answers to all your questions are to be found within this viewing. The wide sweep of your history is the first step in a process to enable you to see those answers.

There are actually four parts to telling your history.

1. Describe your story on paper in words.
2. Tell another person your story and discuss it with them.
3. Describe your history on paper in stick pictures.
4. Tell another person your history and discuss it.

Yes, it sounds redundant, but trust the process, remember? There is an important reason for doing it this way, even if it is not clear to you right now.

1. Describe the story on paper in words.

This account of your life story is told in yearly increments. You describe a year of your life at a time using bullet statements in order from childhood to the present.

A bullet statement is a summary of events reduced to about five to ten words.

The maximum per year is three lines of no more than ten words each. This is one line for each major event of that year. Trust me, you don't need more than three major events in a year. If you think you do, then pick the three most important. Write NO paragraphs. Of course, the statements must make sense.

It is essential you be as straight and honest as you possibly can about this. Do not sugarcoat the experiences. I'll give you an example.

The central event of my life at age 31 was to go from working as a secretary to being a housewife. I can put it in a bullet statement with no sugarcoat like this:

Age 31:   Fired from secretary job. Felt worthless.
          Became housewife to drink.

See how it works? This one statement summarizes an entire year.

Work at condensing your bullet statements while keeping the meaning clear. When you finish this exercise, it should not be more than four to five pages long. You can type a rough draft, if you like, but when you're ready for the final copy, please handwrite it. You'll feel much more connected to the events when you write them. Double space and skip extra lines in between entries you don't remember well to allow space for later recall.

You will probably remember more things as you progress on this historical journey. Don't judge the value or lack of value of the tidbits that come out. At this point you can't see where this process is taking you and therefore it is important not to discard things along the way. You can't know, at this point, what will be important and what will not be important.

Start with your birth. You won't have any remembrance of the circumstances of your birth but make an entry about what you know from family stories or what have you guessed. You'd be surprised at the useful information you find out with that very first entry.

When starting this exercise, many people make the mistake of thinking the only important events relate to drinking, drugging or acting out. Not so. This is your life story. Your addiction is a part of your history but it's only a part. This exercise requires you to remember major events in your life. They may or may not be related to your addiction.

The chronological nature of this exercise is very important. People tend to remember things in separate compartments, never really seeing the connection between 1986's events and those of 1987. Go through the exercise year by year.

Another helpful idea to pursue, there may be relatives or safe friends around who could answer some of your questions. Such potentially helpful people are not readily available to everyone, but if so, they can be a great source of information. For more recent times a spouse, friend, or significant other may have clear recollections. If you are unable to find information on what occurred in a specific year make the entry saying:

Age ___ This year is missing from my life."

2. Tell another person your story and discuss it.

Once you have put together the final draft of your history in chronological order and expressed it in bullet statements, then you are ready to tell the story verbally to someone else and to discuss it.

You may choose to pair up with only one of the group members to tell your story if you are working on this project in a group. However, many people tell their entire group the story. Either method has benefits but I prefer telling a larger group if possible. Choose one or more trusted people in recovery.

As you tell the story aloud more information will come. You will gather yet other vital pieces of the pattern that may have eluded you at first. **WRITE IT DOWN.** Don't forget to do that. The pieces that come to you as you tell the story aloud may be more important than you think. If you haven't written them down, they may well be lost again.

After you have described your life year by year the best way you can, discuss patterns you and your listening partner(s) notice. Make a separate note of those patterns.You will incorporate the information in another step.

The value of your story in this process may not be clear now so keep all this written work together for later reference.

3. Describe each bullet statement of your history on paper in stick pictures.

Don't try to be an artist here. Use a dark writing felt pen. You can use colors, different widths of pens or even crayons to make your message clear. This method is designed to help you connect with your life events at a different level. The process helps put your history into perspective, reduce shame and help you make progress in grieving losses.

Take the entries and major recollections from the writing and telling of your history, and draw a picture to represent each entry. You may want to get some butcher paper or continuous feed computer paper for this project. It is best to have the drawings on a connected piece of paper. With butcher paper you can roll up in a scroll whatever sections you aren't using and make the project more manageable. If you can't locate butcher paper or continuous feed computer paper, use sheets of notebook paper and tape them together to make a continuous roll.

The act of making pictures to correspond with words usually has an impact that can't be achieved by other means. For one thing, many people think in pictures. While you may not remember the words of your history, the pictures of your history tend to flash up during the enhanced recovery work.

4. Show another person this picture story and discuss it.

Do this with a second individual whom you trust or with a group of people. Telling the story in a safe group setting gives you the best impact on your recovery. Take out the history in pictures and if possible tack it to the wall all the way around the room.

This second time through your life is deeper, touches more feelings and the pictures capture in images what you carry around with you. It helps to integrate your life in a cohesive, complete way.

Life and Addiction History Example
Barbara P.

Age 3   Mysteriously broke my collar bone. No explanation from family about how it happened.

Age 5   My nose was broken. No explanation and I don't remember.

Age 7   Parents were drinking and fighting lots. I was afraid my Mom would run off my Dad. Mom had a black eye once. No explanation.

Age 8   I have no memory of this year at all.

Age 9   Dad left me.

Age 10   Moved out of our house into apartment. I hated it.

Age 13   Started Jr. High School. I didn't fit in.
           I had a beer with a friend.
           Felt relaxed for the first time in years.
           Got my first boyfriend.
           Drinking pattern began.
           1 or 2 beers, 2 X a month.

Age 14   Parents divorced. My Mom finally ran off my Dad forever.
           Drinking increased. 2 beers, 4 X a month.

Age 15   Date rape. My first sexual experience. I was drunk. Told nobody. It was my fault.

Age 16   After getting sick from hangover I decided not to drink again. That lasted three months until my boyfriend beat me up and "had" me.

Age 17   Stopped drinking again. Quit for 2 years. Did well in school. Graduated early.

Age 18   Went to A&M Univ. for 2 years. Loved it

96

	at first. Studied hard.
Age 19	Everybodying was partying. I was mad because I couldn't so I decided I didn't really need to stop drinking. Drank 3 beers a night, 3 X a week.
Age 20	Flunked out. Went to work as a clerk. Felt humiliated and worthless. Drinking 6 beers a night, 3-4 X a week.
Age 21	Moved to Chicago. Thought life would be better. It was only colder, not better. Began using marijuana. Drinking about the same amount, too.
Age 22	Mom got sick with leukemia. I'm the only one left to take care of her. I got stuck with it. Felt angry and martyred. Drank more than ever. She drank with me. Drank 6 beers a night, 6 X a week
Age 23	More of same. Got new boyfriend, Ronnie. I was crazy about him. He had good grass. Two joints a day, 6 beers a night 6 X a week.
Age 24	Life is a circle of taking care of Mom, drinking and smoking. I thought I'd found a stable guy. I run them all off after a while. I tried everything I could to hang on. Same amount of grass and alcohol.
Age 25	In a blackout I got my finger broken. Never knew how.

	Mother died.
	3 joints a day and ½ case of beer daily.
Age 26	Desperate, miserable, wanted to die.
	Finally decided to get help.
	Went to AA. Found Mr. Right.
	Stayed sober for 3 months.
Age 29	Back in AA.
	Getting Relapse Prevention Treatment.

Three reasons why you believe you can't do this exercise.

Let's review why you may believe you can't do this exercise. I suspect you believe you have at least some of these reasons. Almost everyone in recovery seems to think this way.

"I can't remember much."

Yes, that may be true but it's important to do it, anyway. There is something about getting into a rhythm with this format that helps unlock memory. People are frequently astounded by the things they remember when they try to put it in chronological order.

Don't worry if you can't remember everything all at once or you feel confused. Start with your birth and your first remembrance (or what you've learned about your early life history) and go forward year by year.

You will begin to remember events you don't recall in the order in which they occurred as you write. Then you can sort the rememberances and write them into the proper place in your history. When an event pops into your memory, ask yourself, "Did this event happen before or after this other milestone." Then write it down in the proper order. It will all start to line up neatly.

For example, you recall you went back to school for two semesters before you got sober the first time but you can't remember what year. Look at what you have written already. Ask yourself, "Did I go back to school before I moved to Chicago or after?" Then ask yourself, "Was that before or after my parents got divorced?" Continue retracing your history until you locate the closest possible year.

Another helpful device to use is visual imagery. With it, it is possible to see the events in your head as if they are on a screen.

Visual imagery is a technique you can learn easily. You are instructed to completely relax your body, close your eyes and visualize the event. (Audio tapes to teach the technique are available at most book stores.)

It works like this: Sit or lie in a comfortable place. Close your eyes. Picture yourself walking in your favorite place and becoming more and more relaxed. Slow your breathing. Try to make the scene as vivid an image in your head as you possibly can. Sense the sounds, smells, and the physical sensations.

When you put yourself in your favorite place and you are very relaxed, then picture the life events that are fuzzy. Try to remember the season it was, any smells or sounds that accompany it, maybe what you were wearing. Make the image as vivid as you can.Then play it forward like a movie film.

A word of caution here. Don't go back and visualize sexual or physical abuse. This can re-traumatize you and that's certainly not the intent here. If you are into a visual imagery experience and traumatic images appear to you, do your best to come back to the here and now.

Feel your chair, open your eyes, notice the room, come back to present, connect with the safety of the place you're in at this moment.You may want to work with a therapist if you have major abuse issues that come in flash-back form.

"Yes but, I've done this lots of times and it doesn't make any difference."

You haven't done this exact assignment as a part of a prescribed process. This format offers a means of integrating life events into a whole picture. It may uncover one of the pieces of your history important to this process but, up to now, you have been unable to "access" by the other histories you have done.

"Yes but, I'm scared of what I might find out."

Yes! Finally, here's what's really going on. You're frightened. Of course, you are! Uncovering parts of yourself long buried can scare the bejabbers out of you. But consider this, you already lived through all these events. They are past and you survived. You are stronger than you think. This review of those events will be worth the fear. It is time to have a talk with yourself.

What exactly do you fear will happen by doing this exercise? How likely is it to really occur? What is the most likely result of doing this exercise? Now quantify your fear. By quantify, I mean give your fear a number value. You do that by asking yourself, "If zero equals no fear at all and ten equals the worst fear imaginable, what is my current fear rating about this exercise?"

If your fear rating is over seven, you need to get some support with this exercise. Look for a partner or a group. Maybe you can enlist your sponsor. In any case, talk about your fear, talk about the rational or irrational nature of it. Talk, talk, talk, until your quantifier for fear is less than seven.

Until the time your fear rating drops below seven, your only assignment is to work at lowering it. Once your fear rating is below seven, begin your history.

This is an excellent technique for dealing with many kinds of fear. Assign a rating to your fear, then ask yourself specific questions about it. Quantify your fear again after you query yourself. If your fear rating remains above seven, don't proceed until you get help. If your fear rating dips below seven, plunge forward.

To accomplish the

Secret Goal

Look inside yourself

CHAPTER 8

RATIONAL THINKING

"I am an old man and have known a great many troubles, but most of them never happened."   Mark Twain

Thus far you have examined your past primary treatment and recovery efforts to shore up your foundation. You have written and retold your history twice. These two efforts helped you take a panoramic view of life events. Then you began looking for recurring patterns. Now, narrow the focus from the sweeping perspective of a wide lens to a close-up lens.

The Role of Rational Emotive Therapy (RET) in Recovery Enhancement

No, I'm not going to go into a long explanation of another model of therapy. However, I am borrowing some helpful concepts from Rational Emotive Therapy, an excellent, effective way of viewing how and why people act as they do. RET asserts that human experiences can logically be divided into these separate and distinct areas. **Situations** in which you find yourself.

Thoughts you have about these situations. **Feelings** produced by these thoughts. And **Urges** or **Actions** that are responses to the three others.

The idea here is you have a constant stream of automatic thoughts going on in your head. You are not even aware of most of them. In addition, RET says that each of these areas logically lead into the next. In other words, Situations lead to Thoughts, which lead to Feelings, and they all lead to Urges or Actions. It is amazing to see things always happen in this order.

People try to make sense out of everything going on in their world. You, therefore, feed yourself a constant stream of thoughts to decide what's happening around you, what it means to you and your personal safety factor regarding the situations. You pay little conscious attention to these thoughts but, unconsciously, you rely heavily upon them.

For example, as you sit in any average home in the U.S., there is a lot of noise going on. You hear a certain sound begin and your subconscious demands, "What is that sound and is it dangerous to me?" (Automatic thought).

Without even consciously knowing it, you supply the answer, "Oh, that's the heater, nothing to worry about." (Another automatic thought).

But let a sound begin that doesn't fit and you lift your head intently, asking yourself, "What is that? Should I worry about it?"

A few seconds later you identify it as a sonic boom and you say to yourself, "It's a sonic boom. No threat, go back to reading your book."

This entire sequence of events often takes place without your conscious awareness. The same kinds of events and subconscious self-talk happens many times each day.

Stop what you are doing right now. What sounds do you hear? Is it the heater or air conditioner? Maybe it's traffic sounds. What had you already decided about those sounds and your vulnerability? Somewhere in your subconscious, you already had automatic thoughts about this and decided whether you needed to flee or fight or if you were safe. You constantly examine your environment and make decisions about what is going on.

Let's look at this phenomena a little closer by using a simple formula. Gorski explains, "Situations lead to thoughts, which lead to feelings which lead to urges or actions." In the example cited, it could be written like this, (provided, of course, you are thinking rationally).

Situation = You hear a sound while reading.

Thought = You ask yourself, "What is that sound

and am I safe?" You think, "It's the heater, I'm okay."

Feeling = This thought leads to feelings such as; secure, safe, comfortable

Urges, Actions = These feelings lead to the action of snuggling in your chair and continuing to read.

See how most of this happens beneath your level of conscious awareness? Don't be fooled, though. The lack of conscious awareness of thoughts is not evidence they don't exist. After all, you have no conscious awareness of the flow of electricity through the walls of your home, but you know it is there.

The example demonstrates how a rational thinking brain operates. Now suppose you are having irrational thoughts. The difference between rational and irrational thoughts is that the rational thoughts are based on facts. There is concrete evidence to support the rational thought. Irrational thoughts are not supported by factual evidence.

However, you may *believe* the thoughts to be completely rational until you take a closer look or someone confronts you.

Now use the same example as above but this time put in irrational automatic thoughts.

Situation = You are sitting in a chair reading and you hear a sound.

Thought = You ask yourself "What is that and am I in danger?" You answer, "It's a bombing raid by the Russians. I knew we couldn't trust them."

This conclusion is irrational because it has no basis in fact. Even though it seems right to you at the time, in reality there is no evidence to support such a deduction.

Feelings = If you think you're in the middle of a bombing raid you feel terror, chaos, panic.
Urges = If these thoughts and feelings are going on in your head and body, you have an urge to find a fallout shelter, hide, run away.
Action = Therefore, you would probably drop your book, scream, grab your family, go try to hide in a safe place.

Imagine the consequences you would reap from such an irrational thought. People would probably doubt your sanity. Your family would wonder if you are using or drinking again. They would certainly think twice about asking your opinions or involving you in discussions.

Eventually you would feel alienated from your family and friends. See the cause/effect relationship? You behave irrationally (the cause) and a distance develops in your relationships (the effect).

These two situations began identically. You heard a sound. The difference in the outcome was caused by your automatic thoughts. One thought was rational (based on evidence) and the other irrational (no evidence to support it).

With rational thinking, life flows more evenly. With irrational thinking, life seems like an emotional roller coaster with no guard rail.

Here is the important part, Guys!

It isn't life situations that get you into trouble.
The situations you face are not "messed up." They are exactly right for you. It is your *thinking* about the situations that is "messed up." You may have no evidence or faulty evidence to support your thoughts if you are thinking irrationally. But you act on them anyway and reap the painful feelings, urges and destructive actions of your irrational ideas.

I admit the above example of irrational thinking is extreme. Let's look at a more common situation and the rational and irrational thinking with which you may respond. The following chart is an observation of what might follow a rational thought about a situation and what might follow the irrational thought about the same situation.

Situation: I go to a 12-step meeting and no one calls on me to share

Rational (based on fact)	Irrational (not based on fact)
Thought = If I really need to share, I can raise my hand but maybe the message is I need to listen tonight.	Thought = The leader has it in for me. There must be something wrong with me. Maybe I need to be smarter (taller, thinner, whatever) before he calls on me.
(From this rational thought I get) Feelings = responsible, comfortable, spiritual.	(From this irrational thought I get) Feelings = Anger, shame, resentment, etc.
(From these feelings I get) Urges = To listen, to be assertive, to participate	(From these feelings I get) Urges = To shut down, to leave the meeting, to stop going to meetings, to avoid the speaker.
(From this urge I take) Action = listening, participating, growing.	(From this urge I take) Action: Say nothing, leave the meeting. Do not receive feedback on my life problems. I begin to abandon my program.

The situation in both examples is the same. The divergence begins with the *thinking*. Your thinking about a situation determines whether you handle it functionally or dysfunctionally. Rational thinking leads to appropriate actions. Irrational thinking leads to inappropriate actions.

This is good news! It means you have the personal power to change every situation from dysfunctional to functional. WOW! The better you can identify and straighten out your automatic thoughts, the better you will be able to handle life situations.

The following chapters will give you more techniques for applying this wonderfully empowering discovery.

Are you Trusting the Process yet?

Life Situations/Problems

Building Blocks of Backtracking

Appropriate Actions	Self-Defeating Actions
↑	↑
Healthy Urges	Unhealthy Urges
↑	↑
Middle-Ground Feelings	Extreme Feelings
↑	↑
Rational Automatic Thoughts	Irrational Automatic Thoughts

CHAPTER 9

BACKTRACKING

"We consume our tomorrows fretting about our yesterdays."   Persius

Patterns of behavior are often bewildering. Your life may seem to be going along smoothly, then suddenly, you realize you are in the midst of a dreadful mess. And darned if you haven't been there before! You can't imagine how you got here again. You may even feel you're being punished or someone else is to blame.

You did your best to cope the last time it happened, but despite your resolve never to get in the same kind of mess again - wham, you're back there. It may be a week later, a month later, or longer since the last time it happened. Regardless, here you are again, smack in the middle of it.

Some life problems are recurring. They are part of a pattern you may or may not recognize. Backtracking is a method of taking a close look at how this pattern happens. It provides a means to identify the step by step process preceding the recurring "mess". This tool has proven a life-saver

112

for many people.

The clarifying technique of Backtracking begins the process of ending repetitive, destructive patterns.

Definition:

Backtracking is a written technique used to help identify specific, dysfuntional patterns of thinking, feeling, urges to act and actions which, if left unchecked, may lead to the dry relapse process.

Potential Situations to Backtrack

☐ Overreactions, (ie. Wanting to beat up the teller at the bank)

☐ Fighting with spouse, boss or sponsor

☐ Becoming defensive

☐ Becoming aggressive

☐ Extremely uncomfortable feelings

☐ Fleeting thoughts of wet relapse

☐ Situations you usually handle well, but this time lost your cool

☐ Sudden rage

☐ Compulsive behaviors surfacing

☐ Obsessive thoughts

☐ Sudden unrealistic euphoria

☐ Offering irrational excuses for behavior

☐ Obsession with others lives/problems

- [ ] Mind racing
- [ ] Change in meeting attendance structure
- [ ] Placing self in high risk situations
- [ ] Dishonesty
- [ ] Lashing out at children or pets
- [ ] Changes in driving habits such as speeding, profanity, aggressiveness
- [ ] Sudden depression
- [ ] Confusion
- [ ] Bewilderment
- [ ] Persistant Post Acute Withdrawal not responding to stress management techniques
- [ ] Any situation in your life you think would benefit from Backtracking. It won't hurt to do extra ones.

Begin your Backtrack by following a specific format:

1. Identify a repeating pattern happening in your life.
2. When it reccurs, use the following Backtracking format. Sit down with paper and pencil and trace all the events that happened before the dysfunctional situation you identified.
3. When you complete the format, you have described all the Dry Relapse Dominos falling in this repetitive pattern. You will know your

thoughts, feelings, urges and what you actually did before you acted out.

Are you are saying to yourself, "I already know that stuff. I am well aware of what my patterns are?" Think again. I guarantee the information you uncover using this format will surprise you.

Many people first think of using this tool for wet relapse episodes. Of course, it's okay to start there. I urge you to do that if you're having difficulty with wet relapse.

More productively, look for patterns happening *before* you act out a wet relapse if you are having dry relapse problems. Remember, you have a dry relapse before a wet one.

Most people tend to focus on the consequences of a dysfunctional event *after* the incident has occurred. Backtracking examines the situation before the dysfunction occurs.

A sample situation will demonstrate for you, step by step, the Backtracking technique.

Jane is an alcoholic. Her first use of the format will be to Backtrack a recurring life problem she has not been able to handle very well. She will begin with the moment she acted out the problem and look back at the preceding

115

few days.

The recurring life problem disrupting to her recovery is identified by her as verbal screaming matches with her spouse.

In her Backtrack, she will trace her situations, thoughts, feelings, urges and actions during the two days before she yelled at him. She will use Stages One, Two and Three of Backtracking to help her.

In the beginning, it doesn't matter whether she believes those situations, thoughts, feelings urges and actions are related to her acting out or not. She will assume for the time being every single thing that happened in the time period just before the yelling match is important.

You can find many answers for your actions and "unsolvable" life-problems if you will approach this technique with an open mind.

You may think many incidents in your day are unrelated to the acting out and consider writing them down as silly. I urge you, do not pass judgment and thereby skip parts. Trust the Process. Visualize everything as important. As the Backtrack evolves, you will understand why.

When discussing Backtracking, where ever you see the phrase, "acting out" it refers to the identified dysfunctional event being traced. Such

116

as "Jane blew up at her spouse."

Stage One of Backtracking
Refer to the chart called *Stage One of Backtracking* on page 118.

At 6:00 PM on Friday Jane went home and screamed at her husband, Bill, letting him have it with both barrels. Now mind you, he irritated her by something he did or did not do, but her reaction was out of proportion to the incident.

The next day, feeling ashamed and mixed up, Jane takes out a sheet of paper and a pencil. She begins to write the outline of a Backtrack using the bell-shaped chart. She writes the acting out description - "Blew up at spouse" - on the lower far right hand corner of the page and then fills in the relevent time slots for the two days before. She will enter the times important to her on the chart.

When Jane has completed her diagram, her Backtrack will be in chronological order from the day or so before the acting out and ending in the actual acting out episode.

Stage 1: Backtracking

Thursday

Friday

Noon

4:00 p.m.

8:00 p.m.

8:00 a.m.

Noon

4:00 p.m.

10:00 a.m.

6:00 p.m.

Blew up at spouse

Stage Two of Backtracking.

Refer to the chart called *Stage Two of Backtracking* on page 121.

Jane next writes down each event she remembers from the past two days in the relevant time frame on her chart.

Friday 4:00 PM   S (situation) = Couldn't concentrate on work, memory shot, thinking fuzzy.

Then she goes to another time period on the sheet.

Friday 8 AM   S = Slept badly, got up late.

She fills in each time frame with whatever was taking place at that time. She doesn't worry about whether or not this event appears to be related to what eventually happened.

Make your statements about the events in short, bullet statements. Take time to think about the event, then write a short summary of it. You'll lose the impact of the format if you write long sentences. Think in short statements.

Jane ends up with a sequence of situations or

events. She did not allow herself to skip time frames.

Never skip time frames, though you can alter the times on the charts to fit your situations. You can add time frames if they seem important.

It is critical to take an accurate look at what was going on in the period just before the acting out. You need at least four or five timed situations in each day in order to get a good "snap shot" of the time period leading up to the acting out.

Stage 2: Backtracking

S=Was tired & skipped mtg.

S=Slept badly, got up late.

S=Others went to lunch without me.

S=Couldn't focus on work, memory shot, thinking fuzzy

BLEW UP AT SPOUSE

8:00 p.m.

4:00 p.m.

Noon

8:00 a.m.

Noon

4:00 p.m.

6:00 p.m.

10: a.m.

Thursday

Friday

S=Couldn't stop thinking about layoff at work

S=Coworker tells me about possible layoff.

S=I compare my work to co-workers & mine is no good

S=Situations, T=Thoughts, F=Feelings, U=Urges to do something, A=Action - what I actually did.

121

Stage Three of Backtracking

Refer to the chart on Page 125, *Stage Three of Backtracking.*

After labeling all the situations, Jane begins to identify her thoughts, feelings and actions or urges taking place during each of the time slots.

Remember the discussion on Rational Emotive Therapy? Here is where you apply it. Each situation in life provokes automatic thoughts. These thoughts lead to feelings leading into urges and then an immediate action. People tend to be unaware of their automatic thinking about everyday life situations. However, knowledge about it is a very important if you are going to change patterns.

Therefore, it is important to identify each of the T-F-U-A'S leading to a reccuring situation.

In Stage Three of Backtracking, go back to each situation on your chart, one at a time. Think about each one. Visualize yourself back in that moment. Recall what you were thinking.

Chances are, if you were in the middle of an acting out episode, your thinking was irrational. Try to pull up in your memory the irrational thoughts you were having. By the way, you may believe your thoughts were not irrational. That's okay. When writing your thoughts on your chart use a "T" followed by a short summary of what you were thinking. *See the chart example.*

Jane began her Stage Two by going back to her chart. Working in chronological order, under each of the situations identified in Stage One she entered her thoughts, feelings, urges and actions.
She then moved to the next occurring event or situation on her bell-shaped chart.
She continued writing in each time frame on her chart, repeating the process of filling in the T-F-U-A's (thoughts, feelings, urges actions).

When you are doing your backtracking chart, if any additional situations occur to you during the procedure, add them to your chart. Frequently the very last thing you remember is critical.

When writing down your feelings, recognize feelings can usually be described with one word. Examples - sad, mad, happy, glad, irritated, furious, comfortable, anxious, worried, calm, generous, powerful, weak, empty, lonely. One word.

If you try to write a feeling with the words, "I felt like . . ." or "I felt that . . ." you are expressing a thought not a feeling. This is an important distinction. You may have to struggle to make certain the feelings section of this exercise is expressed as feelings rather than thoughts, but it is very important you spend the time to do this well.

Refer to the Chart on page 125, *Stage Three of Backtracking* for the almost finished product.

The last task for Jane is the evaluation of what she has learned from this exercise.

Stage 2: Backtracking

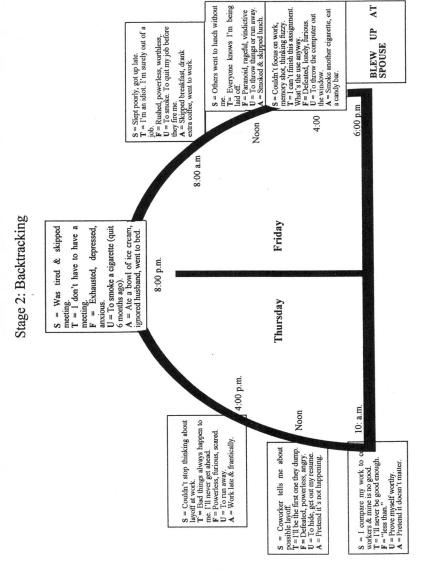

S = Was tired & skipped meeting.
T = I don't have to have a meeting.
F = Exhausted, depressed, anxious.
U = To smoke a cigarette (quit 6 months ago).
A = Ate a bowl of ice cream, ignored husband, went to bed.

8:00 p.m.

8:00 a.m.

S = Slept poorly, got up late.
T = I'm an idiot. I'm surely out of a job.
F = Rushed, powerless, worthless.
U = To smoke. To quit my job before they fire me.
A = Skipped breakfast, drank extra coffee, went to work.

S = Others went to lunch without me.
T = Everyone knows I'm being laid off.
F = Paranoid, rageful, vindictive
U = To throw things or run away.
A = Smoked & skipped lunch.

Noon

4:00

S = Couldn't focus on work, memory shot, thinking fuzzy.
T = I can't finish this assignment. What's the use anyway.
F = Defeated, lonely, furious.
U = To throw the computer out the window.
A = Smoke another cigarette, eat a candy bar.

6:00 p.m

BLEW UP AT SPOUSE

Thursday   Friday

4:00 p.m.

S = Couldn't stop thinking about layoff at work.
T = Bad things always happen to me. I'll never get ahead.
F = Powerless, furious, scared.
U = To run away.
A = Work late & frantically.

Noon

10: a.m.

S = Coworker tells me about possible layoff.
T = I'll be the first one they dump.
F = Defeated, powerless, angry.
U = To hide, get out my resume.
A = Pretend it's not happening.

S = I compare my work to c[...]workers & mine is no good.
T = I'll never be good enough.
F = "less than."
U = Prove myself worthy.
A = Pretend it doesn't matter.

S=Situations, T=Thoughts, F=Feelings, U=Urges to do something, A=Action - what I actually did.

125

The Meaning of the Backtrack

Read the Stage Three Backtracking Chart from the left to right. Follow the chronological sequence.

This is the story of Jane, who came to a session and said, "My husband is driving me crazy."

She then described how he, "Went off on me Friday night for no reason and then when I yelled back the whole thing was a nightmare."

She could not see a connection between her overreaction to her husband and what had happened to her in the two days before the yelling match. She didn't see a pattern.

It is important to know Jane had stopped smoking a few months before this. When she reported smoking as an event in her Backtrack it was actually a relapse into that addictive behavior. Quite a difference from just "having a cigarette".

When you read her Backtrack, what stands out? What patterns of thinking, feeling and acting are there? Did you notice the recurring theme of food (or lack thereof), sugar and caffeine?

Until she did this backtrack, Jane didn't have a clue about these patterns in her behavior. Nor did she realize how deeply frightened she was by the potential layoff at work. (The layoff, by the way, turned out to be only gossip.)

Look at all the Thoughts. Can you see the irrational nature of her thinking? Imagine the pain she was feeling as these thoughts crowded her mind.

Now look at all the Actions. See how she never guessed these events to be related? Yet, when she wrote them down she began to see a distinct pattern. She also became aware of places to intervene in this pattern.

She could have known by Thursday she was in serious trouble if she had an early dry relapse warning system in place. Then she could have chosen to take different actions during Thursday evening and changed the outcome dramatically.

By Backtracking Jane realized her thoughts such as, "The worst things always happen to me." were signs of her dysfunction needing urgent attention. Her intervention was to call her sponsor to discuss the thought whenever it occurred. This simple action worked. It was the exact intervention needed. It helped Jane get a rational perspective and prevented the downhill slide into acting out and its consequences.

The Benefits of Backtracking

Backtracking is a powerful tool enabling you to better understand your day to day behavior. People often have the idea routine daily actions are unrelated to the other events of their life. Backtracking is clear, undeniable proof of the connectedness of all the realms of your life. Use it to trace back life events and find the source of difficulties. It is an incredibly empowering tool. What's more, it doesn't take a genius to do it.

Backtrack with your sponsor or someone else you trust. If you are having difficulty with irrational thoughts, you probably need an objective person to assist you. But, in the absence of a helping person, Backtracking can definitely be worked out alone.

Denial falls away when you trace and write down your sequential situations, thoughts, feelings, urges and actions. You can finally see the whole process of going from a functional track to acting out behavior. The triggers, set ups and patterns stare you in the face. They are impossible to deny because, after all, *you* wrote them down on that piece of paper.

Backtracking is an important step in the process of Recovery Enhancement. By identifying patterns in a logical way, reducing denial, and increasing awareness of reccurences in your patterns, you introduce a catalyst for positive change.

Picture dominos set on end in a row, one

behind the other. With a flick of the finger on the first domino, one by one, they begin to fall.

By using Backtracking, you can identify each of the personal dominos that can fall, one by one, leading to your next acting out episode.

I did not say you can eradicate these patterns immediately. I am introducing a way to know more about the process of dysfunction. Over time and with practice you can begin to eliminate the patterns. Don't expect life-time responses to disappear with your first, "AHA!," about them.

Trust the process.

How to Backtrack

A. Identify your acting out episode.
B. Record the time and date of your acting out episode.
C. Write down key times for the previous two days i.e. 8 a.m., noon, 4 p.m., 8 p.m. You choose the relevant times.
D. Identify and record situtations occurring in each of the key times.
E. After all of the situations are recorded, describe in writing corresponding T-F-U-A's (thoughts, feelings, urges, actions) beneath each situation.
F. When you have the above completed, ask yourself, "What patterns do I see? What stands out?"
G. Make a check mark by any of your thoughts that now seem irrational. (Make sure you have a clear definition of irrational in your mind.)
H. Circle any potential signs of dry relapse that stand out.
I. Reinforce your newly learned skill over and over.

Backtracking Exercise

The way to feel the effectiveness of this tool is - you guessed it - do it.

Team up with your sponsor or your Recovery Enhancement partner(s). Decide to work on a recent situation when you acted in a self-destructive way. I'm not talking about using or drinking. You are looking for patterns that set you up for a wet relapse and these are found in dry relapse experiences.

Use the method described in this chapter for your Backtrack.

If you prefer, the workbook contains a "Template" for the Backtracking exercise. The Template has blank spaces you fill in with your information.

When you have completed your Backtracking exercise, it's important to note certain things about it.

1. **Patterns.** What events in this exercise happen frequently and seem very familiar?

2. **Denial.** What awareness has come from this exercise? Which events didn't seem related before beginning the exercise but are now undeniably related.

3. **Triggers.** Identify the precipitating event

kicking off the dysfunction.

4. **Irrational Thoughts**.What automatic thoughts contributed to the problem and is there another way to look at them?

5. **Identify the Relapse Dominos**. In different words from those used in the backtracking, describe the step by step process of this dry relapse.

Complete at least four Backtracks on different life problems to obtain the best picture of the process.

Backtracking Helpful Hints

- ▸ This is a chronological record.
- ▸ You are on a fact-finding mission only.
- ▸ Everything happening during the time period is important.
- ▸ Do not worry about meanings or the relative importance of events until the end of the exercise.
- ▸ You must find patterns yourself.
- ▸ Backtracking can be done with either an individual or a group.
- ▸ The important information will stand out when the record is completed.
- ▸ Reinforce your skill by repetition.

CHAPTER 10

NAMING DRY RELAPSE DOMINOS

"What each man does is based not on direct and certain knowledge, but on pictures made my himself or given to him."   Walter Lippman

At this point, you have revisited your foundations in recovery and looked at the wide-screened picture of your life. You recognize the best way to enhance recovery is by eliminating the repetitive patterns of self-destructive behavior.

Then you narrowed the focus to look at specific patterns involved in your dry relapses by completing at least four Backtracking exercises on different acting out episodes . . . recurring life problems you didn't handle well.

This chapter will teach you how to use the completed work from the previous chapters to nail down the exact process leading to dry relapse.

A frequent problem in recovery work is the lack of a thorough examination prior to attempting major change. Until you know the exact source of the problem how can you solve it? You will end up changing the symptom instead of the disease.

Eliminating the cough without treating the pneumonia results in a failure to cure.

With the completion of the work up to now, you have a good basic knowledge of your patterns. The following chapters will show you how to intervene in these patterns and successfully substitute healthier ways of living.

I recommend you don't go further until all the exercises from the preceding chapters are complete. A process does not work well unless it is completed in order, one step at a time. So go on, do your four Backtracks. I'll be right here waiting. Hurry back!

Dry Relapse Dominos are the concrete symptoms of dysfunction, our individualized signs along the Dry Relapse Slide. They are specific situations, thoughts, feelings, urges or actions appearing in a sequential order. These Dominos are sneaky little guys and may appear completely unrelated to your dysfunction. Don't be deceived, looking "unrelated" is their smoke screen.

Dry Relapse Dominos are different for everyone. Use the format described in this chapter to uncover yours.

My personal Dominos probably aren't the same as yours. Though there may be some similarities, you and I are different people. Your dominos can trace the path from a healthy, successful recovery lifestyle to a state of being miserable enough to consider using alcohol, drugs or even suicide.

Remember the analogy of dominos in a row? This chapter helps you name and recognize your identifying signs on the face of each domino leading you along your personal path to anguish.

Identifying your signs can empower you to notice when they occur so you can intervene. Intervention lets you eliminate some of the dominos from a long row. Removal of these dominoes can *stop* the entire domino effect, or process. Taking away dominos prevents the ones at the end of the row from falling.

Unfortunately, many people don't know they are involved in a process of dry relapse, much less how to interrupt the process. Considering the "smoke-screen" nature of these Dominos, how do you know enough to stop any of them? You don't until you identify each of your Dry Relapse Dominos.

This technique for using Relapse Dominos to help you prevent relapse evolved from the work of Don Travins, Executive Director of Sunrise House, a residential treatment facility in California specializing in treatment for relapse-prone individuals.

Don's creative and nurturing style empowered

his staff and patients to put their heads together to find new techniques and powerful methods to prevent relapse. Many kudos to you, Don.

Recovery Enhancement suggests you:
1. Know there is a dry relapse process. That a domino effect exists.
2. Identify what your personal process looks like.
3. Identify your specific Dry Relapse Dominoes and label each of them.
4. Look for and adopt the Universal Principles available to you from your life's problems.
5. Develop a plan to interrupt the domino effect as early as possible in the process.
6. Be alert for Dry Relapse Dominoes you have not identified yet.

Dry Relapse Dominos

I work late and frantically.
T= I must work like a dog or they'll fire me.
F= I feel fear, stress.
U= I want to run away.
A= I try harder.

I can't stop thinking about work.
T= If I lose my job I'll never get another one.
F= I feel terror, jittery.
U= I have an urge to do anything to keep it.
A= I drive like a maniac.

137

The identification of your Dry Relapse Dominos depends upon your participation in the process of Recovery Enhancement. You must draw from your completed exercises to get an accurate picture of your personal dominos. Don't just guess at what they are. If you don't do the work, you will not gain the benefit. You must identify many possible dominos, narrow down the list and then, finally, put them in order.

You may ask, "So what exactly does a domino list look like?".

Example

Look at the Stage 3 Backtracking chart on page 125. This is Jane's chart and it has an abundance of possible dominos. Find them by looking at the Situations listed in each time sequence. They are (in chronological order):

1. I compare my work to co-worker's and mine is no good.
2. Co-worker tells me about possible layoff.
3. Couldn't stop thinking about layoff at work.
4. Was tired and skipped meeting.
5. Slept badly, got up late.
6. Others went to lunch without me.
7. Couldn't concentrate on work, memory shot, thinking fuzzy.
8. Blew up at Spouse.

Several of these events or situations are clear indicators Jane's dysfunctional pattern is in full swing. Which ones apply to you? Write them down as Dry Relapse Dominos even if there is only a slight chance they are warning signs for one of your reccuring patterns. Writing them down doesn't set them in concrete, you can always discard what is not relevant.

Which situations will you choose? For an example, I'll take the following situations from Jane's Backtrack list to make her Dry Relapse Dominos:

1. I compare my work to co-worker's and mine is no good.

Maybe in your case, "self" can substitute for work.

2. Couldn't stop thinking about (layoff at) work.

If you take out the words "layoff at" from the above Situation, this Dry Relapse Domino would have a more universal application in life.

3. Was tired & skipped meeting.
4. Slept badly, got up late.
5. Others went to lunch without me .

Add the words, "and my feelings were hurt" for a more accurate picture of the situation.

6. Couldn't concentrate on work, memory shot, thinking fuzzy.
7. Blew up at spouse.

See how this process works? Most of the situations from the Backtrack make excellent Dry Relapse Dominos with a little fine tuning. (When you "fine tune" situations, be sure you are making them more general rather than more specific.)

Can you follow the progression of events in the Dry Relapse Dominos? In particular, note the way the sequence starts off small and builds to a crisis.

Now review the Stage 3 Backtracking chart again. Read the *Actions* from each time sequence.

- ▸ Pretended it doesn't matter that I don't measure up.
- ▸ Pretended it's not happening.
- ▸ Worked late and frantically.
- ▸ Ate a bowl of ice cream, ignored husband, went to bed.
- ▸ Skipped breakfast, drank extra coffee, went to work.
- ▸ Smoked a cigarette, skipped lunch.

▸ Smoked another cigarette, ate candy bar.

Let's select some of the Actions to make helpful dominoes for Jane. These are taken directly from her Backtrack in chronological order. From these *Actions* you can pick the following to make Dry Relapse Dominos. (Notice the emphasis on food revealed in Jane's Backtrack.)

8.   Pretend it doesn't matter that I, or believe that I, don't measure up.
9.   Pretend it's not happening.
10. Work late and frantically.
11. Eat a bowl of ice cream, ignore husband, go to bed.
12. Skip breakfast, drink extra coffee, go to work.
13. Smoke a cigarette, skip lunch.
14. Smoke another cigarette and eat candy bar (add "*in the afternoon*")

So far, you have examined only the *Actions* and *Situations* from Jane's Backtrack and you already have 14 potential Dry Relapse Dominos.

Examine the Thoughts, Feelings, and Urges of Jane's Backtrack to obtain a full list of Dry Relapse Dominos. Add up *your* data. See the Dry Relapse Dominos you get from one Backtrack.

I have added a few more of the thoughts, feelings, and urges that stand out and complete the picture of Jane's backtrack.

Arrange the thoughts, feelings, urges in chronological order, (a critical procedure) so they come out S-T-F-U-A, going from time sequence to time sequence.

Dry Relapse Dominos taken from Backtrack

1. I compare myself to others and decide I'm no good.
2. I pretend it doesn't matter I believe I don't measure up.
3. I feel defeated, powerless and angry.
4. I pretend it's not happening.
5. I can't stop thinking about work.
6. I work late and frantically.
7. I have an urge to run away.
8. I'm tired and skip meeting I need badly.
9. I have an urge to relapse in smoking.
10. I eat a bowl of ice cream at bedtime and ignore spouse.
11. I sleep badly, get up late.
12. I think, " I'm an irresponsible idiot."
13. I skip breakfast, drink extra coffee, go to work.
14. Others go to lunch without me, my feelings are hurt.

15. I feel paranoid, rageful and vindictive. I relapse with a cigarette, skip lunch.
16. I can't concentrate on work, memory shot, thinking fuzzy.
17. I feel defeated, lonely and hopeless.
18. I eat a candy bar in the afternoon.
19. I blow up at Spouse and believe it's his fault.

On this list notice that some of the verbs have been changed from past to present tense. For instance, instead of "ate ice cream", it says "eat ice cream." This is an important part of this format. Convert your Domino Names this way.

In addition, each Dry Relapse Domino is formulated with a whole sentence. Later on, you won't have all your dominos in one package so each Domino must make sense all by itself.

The above list is an excellent word picture of Jane's dysfunctional reccuring pattern. It is not a description of your pattern.

You can't understand this process by osmosis. Pull information from your Backtracks to make your own list or the exercise will be ineffective.

Example of
Naming the Dominos

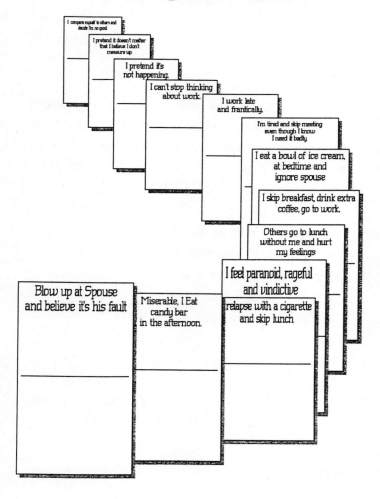

Add the Thoughts, Feelings, Urges, and Actions (T-F-U-A's)

Assume that each one of the Dominos you have selected is a situation and each one will be a symptom on the pathway to dysfunction. You need to generalize now. You are no longer talking about one specific incident. You're going to be looking at overall life patterns. So step back from your individual, completed Backtracks. Look at the global picture.

The next step is to add the T-F-U-A's that may follow each of the dominos. Some of them will be already worked out in your Backtrack, but others won't.

Need an example? Each of the following T-F-U-A's is taken directly from the list of Dry Relapse Dominos named on Jane's list.

Domino: I pretend it doesn't matter I believe I don't measure up.

T = *When this is happening, I think,* "I must not notice my pain."

F = *When I'm thinking this, I feel* stressed, anxious

U = *This gives me the urge to* get busy on many projects to prevent noticing my pain.

A = *What I actually do next* is become over involved in projects for which I don't have time.

Domino: I feel defeated, powerless and angry.

T = *When this is happening, I think,* " There's no way out of this mess."

F = *When I am thinking this, I feel* trapped, anxious, fearful

U = *This gives me the urge to* quit my job and run away.

A = *What I actually do next is* keep trying to perform the impossible.

Domino: I pretend it's not happening.

T = *When this is happening, I think,* "If I ignore it, it will go away."

F = *When I'm thinking this way, I feel* confused, bewildered, anxious.

U = *This gives me the urge to* act out sexually.

A = *What I actually do next* is binge on chocolate bars.

Can you see how this works?

Names and T-F-U-A's
of Dry Relapse Dominos

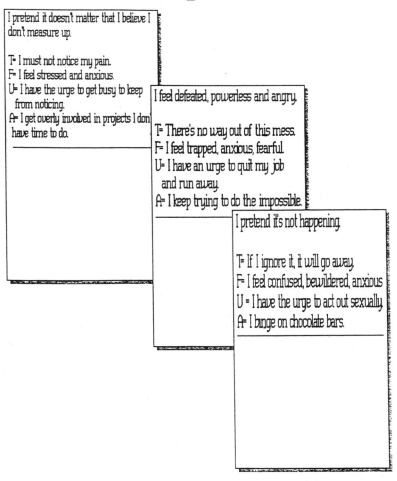

I pretend it doesn't matter that I believe I don't measure up.

T= I must not notice my pain.
F= I feel stressed and anxious.
U= I have the urge to get busy to keep from noticing.
A= I get overly involved in projects I don't have time to do.

I feel defeated, powerless and angry.

T= There's no way out of this mess.
F= I feel trapped, anxious, fearful.
U= I have an urge to quit my job and run away.
A= I keep trying to do the impossible.

I pretend it's not happening.

T= If I ignore it, it will go away.
F= I feel confused, bewildered, anxious
U = I have the urge to act out sexually.
A= I binge on chocolate bars.

Pile up the Domino Cards

Once you have a long list of possible Dominos from several backtracks, put the list in chronological order. Obtain a stack of 5" x 8" unruled index cards. Make them into Dominos by turning each card so the 5" part is the width and the 8" part is the length. You will be writing across the 5" part of the card.

On the top half of one side of each card, write a Dry Relapse Domino's situation or event and it's T-F-U-A.

Later in this exercise, you will add information to the front bottom and on the back of each Domino card.

Imagine each card represents one of those dominos that could fall along the pathway to your Wet Relapse. Ideally, you will have a stack of at least 20 - 30 Dry Relapse Domino cards.

Put the Dominos in Order

Here's the fun part. I recommend you do this part with an REP partner or another interested person.

Sit down on the floor or use a large flat desk or table surface. Review the Domino cards, reading them aloud one at a time, including the names (situations or events), Thoughts, Feelings, Urges and Actions.

Some of the Domino cards will clearly and obviously be duplicates. Stack the duplicates together with a paper clip and set them aside.

Sort through the rest of the Domino cards and arrange them in order of the occurrence of the situation written on each one.

At first, this sorting may be a little confusing but you'll get it as you go along. As you hold one card in your hand, ask yourself, "Does this domino fall before or after the one I just laid down? When you have finished, you will end up with a line of dominos (index cards) giving you a clear description from start to finish of how your Dry Relapse process happens.

Often, you may find there is one or two dominos not on cards. Maybe something you didn't recall at first but now, for instance, you know happened between Domino number seven and Domino number eight. No problem. Just write another Domino card for the missing step and insert it in its place between Domino seven and Domino eight.

For example, your Domino number seven is, "I think of lies to tell." Your Domino number eight is, "My friend realizes I have lied to her and is mad."

It's clear that something had to happen between your *thinking* of telling a lie and your friend's anger because you lied to her.

Of course! You must have actually told a lie. So you write another Domino card for "I tell a lie" and insert it between the two existing cards.

By inserting the new card you have a complete picture of how the process actually happened. Aim for this complete picture when writing your domino cards.

Once you've got the Dry Relapse Dominos named and the cards in order, then number the cards on the front upper right corner so they can be kept in order should you drop the stack. Use a pencil for this because you may think of another card to insert later.

Herald House/Independence Press publishes what is called Relapse Warning Sign Cards. This set of cards gives you a very organized way to keep track of the Dry Relapse Dominos. They are pre-printed and ask you critical questions about your "warning signs", including a place to write management techniques. Call for information about price and how to order them by calling the Herald House number in the bibliography.

Your Turn

Pull out the four or more Backtracking exercises you have completed. You are going to make dominos from your own Backtracks.

First, review the Situations, then Actions, then Thoughts, Feelings and Urges. Are they concrete and clear enough to make good Dominos? Remember, when you use your situations, actions, thoughts, feeling and urges on dominoes, each piece of information will be independent of the other information on that Backtracking Exercise.

Be certain to make whole sentences with complete thoughts using the present tense.

Don't make decisions or judgments about whether or not you believe every situation, thought, feeling or urge is *your* Domino at this stage of the process. Trust that since the process has revealed this data it is leading in the right direction. For now, you are only collecting facts. Later, you will sort them out.

Once you have located potential Dry Relapse Dominos, write them in the present tense and in whole sentences beginning with the word "I".

Remember, it's not what others are doing that is a Dry Relapse Sign for you, it's what you are doing. Thus, all your Dry Relapse Dominos start with "I".

Sometimes, your behavior is your reaction to

151

another person's conduct , but it is still expressed as an "I" statement. For example, "I get angry when John Doe goes near my wife."

Record each Dry Relapse Domino on a 5 x 8 index card.

Write out the Thoughts, Feelings, Urges and Actions for each Domino, using the name of the Domino as the Situation.

Arrange your dominos in chronological order. Look for duplicates and combine them into one domino

It is probable many new dominos will be recalled during the work to come. Identify and write them down in your binder. You'll need them later.

The Trust the Process Workbook provides exercises to help you accomplish the above tasks.

CHAPTER 11

DEALING WITH PROBLEMS

"I know God will not give me anything I can't handle. I just wish He didn't trust me so much."
Mother Teresa

Some of you began your recovery journey with the idea that sobriety would bring a life free of problems. Of course, it wasn't long before you understood your folly.

I must admit, it came as a great surprise to me to find out the situations of my world weren't all that different in recovery. With, of course, the notable exception that I no longer had the complications of active addiction.

In abstinence, there continues to be money problems, social problems, relationship problems, parent problems, children problems and job trouble. The bad guys of the universe have not disappeared.

Recovering people are not free of problems. Not by any measure. You are, however, freed from the bondage of your addiction. You can now use all your personal resources to solve your problems.

In this chapter I will discuss several techniques

for dealing with problems. Some of them are in the form of a series of questions. I suggest you work this chapter by taking pen and paper and first write down, then apply the methods to your current life problems right away. Research indicates that if newly learned skills are not used immediately you are unlikely to integrate them into your life.

Do you have that pen and paper? Let's explore.

Why do I have problems?

This is one of those universal questions requiring a book of its own. But, try on this idea. Your difficulties can help you stretch and grow. The way you look at the world is altered whenever you successfully deal with a difficult situation. A part of you says, "I dealt with that okay. Maybe I can also deal with the next trouble to come my way."

You develop reliance on principles and values such as honesty, integrity, and responsibility. You are, thereby, mending your Soul Wounds.

What are the rewards of keeping problems?

One reason it is so difficult to solve problems is because you have inherent benefits when you keep them. You may scoff at the idea you are benefiting from being miserable, but it's true.

For one thing, by staying stuck you don't have to grow and deal with the discomfort accompanying change. You can continue to avoid looking at the underlying issues of your life.

You never have to notice you give all your power away to another if you stay focused on the idea that the other person is *making* you miserable. Nor will you notice you are scared to death of finding your inner strength.

What is the problem?

You're not likely to solve a problem until you state the problem clearly. So, write it down. You used this method in Backtracking, remember?

Write down all the thoughts you have about the problem at hand. It's okay to ramble. Just write! In particular, include the "must", "should", "can't", and "aught to" statements playing their parts in your problem.

Once your writing is complete, go back and summarize what you just wrote. A problem can be reduced to one sentence if it is really understood. Think in terms of the bullet statements explained in the Backtracking exercise. Make your sentences short and to the point.

By the way, the definition of your problem may change when you finish the exercises in this chapter.

Once you have reduced a problem to a bullet sentence, fill in the following blanks.

The problem I am dealing with is . . .
My automatic thought about this problem is, "I should (or must, or can't)". . .
When I think this thought I feel . . .
When I have these thoughts and feelings about this problem, I have an urge to . . .
What I will do instead is . . .

Whose problem is it?

It's amazing how much energy is spent on problems that don't belong to you. It's common to get absorbed in someone else's life issues, providing you with an easy, socially acceptable way to avoid your own matters. Taking responsibility for another's problems often gives you unnecessary pain and delays your own growth.

I'm not suggesting you never empathize or help others, just don't make their problems your problem. Everyone must own their own problems in order to solve them. You are *stealing away* a person's opportunity to learn the lessons needed to work out problems if you take reponsibility for them.

Your efforts to solve another's problem means that person will have to experience the same problem again, maybe in another, more difficult form than this one.

In fact, to interfere in someone else's problem is really a selfish act. You foster within yourself the irrational thought. "I can't tolerate my own discomfort about what they are experiencing."

Look inward and deal with the reason their discomfort is so hard for you to bear. Don't use their pain as justification for stealing their chance to grow and learn from their pain.

A short cut to deciding whether the problem is yours or not is to ask yourself, "Are the upset feelings I have about my own or someone else's pain?" It is not your problem if the answer is, "someone else's pain."

This does not mean, however, you cannot be sensitive to another's pain. You *can* acknowledge their problem and their pain without taking possession of it.

Empathy is a feeling of rapport, of knowing and understanding another's position. Strive for empathic feelings, but understand there is a great deal of difference between feeling empathic toward others and taking on their problems as your own.

Give affirmations instead of stealing another's growth. "Yes, I see you are in pain." and, "Yes, I believe you are are capable of finding the right solutions for yourself." And, "Yes, anytime you want to talk to me about this problem, you can call." This way you give them a lifelong gift of self-empowerment to help them help themselves rather than satisfy your selfish need for distraction.

Do you feel defensive?

Defensiveness is feeling the need to protect a vulnerable area. It is a part of the fight or flight phenomenon - a part of your brain believes you are in physical danger. When a severe threat is perceived in the subconscious you become defensive.

A defensive response triggers a sudden increase in adrenaline resulting in rapid breathing and pulse rate, loud and/or pressured speech and an increased intensity of activity. You may offer excuses to justify your position. You have a big investment in convincing another person you are right.

The recipient of the defensive response may think, "Why is my friend so upset about this? The issue at hand is either a fact or it is not."

Of course, if the recipient is defensive too, you

can have a whole new ballgame. The situation escallates and soon the origin of the discussion is lost.

Most of the time, you don't recognize your defensiveness. It is such an automatic response that you simply don't notice it. However, knowing how to recognize your defensive behavior gives you great power. Use it to manage and solve problems.

There is likely to be underlying issues involved when you are defensive. You are not only defending the situation at hand, you are probably defending an underlying issue.

For example, go back to the situation when my sponsor embarrassed me in front of our 12-step group. I felt hurt as well as angry.

If I confronted her directly, I would say, "I felt hurt when you said what you did." Instead, I react defensively. I say nothing and avoid her and my 12-step group. I pretend it doesn't matter what she says, but inside I fume and build resentment.

Finally, my sponsor calls me again. She says, "How are you? Where have you been? I'm worried about you."

My defenses go sky high. I squirm in my chair, my heart pounds. I begin to rattle a series of excuses about why I haven't been doing what I need to do. Some of my statements may even be outright lies. I describe all the baseball games my kids had, all the PTA meetings, how my dog has PMS, how I've been sick with a cold. What I don't say is, "You hurt my feelings."

Defensiveness keeps me from facing the issue assertively. I avoid dealing directly with the source of my pain.

All this craziness is subconsciously fueled by my survival rule that says, "I can't tell others when I'm angry or else they'll leave me."

The more defensive I become, the deeper I am mired in the problem. Now I have lied to her. And I have to remember this lie because she may mention it again. What if she says something about my imaginary cold in front of others? Then I'll have to lie to them. What a mess.

People seldom recognize the importance of defensive situations. They deny them or ignore them. You can open the door to resolution of the situations by recognizing when you are feeling and behaving defensively. The better you become at knowing when you're defensive, the sooner you can get to the underlying problem. In the example, the time and energy I used to create and defend all my excuses was sheer waste.

Using the same example but from a different perspective, look at what happens when a person recognizes their defensive behavior.

As in the first example, my sponsor calls me and asks, "Where have you been?"

I hadn't consciously realized I'd been avoiding her. I truly thought, "I am too busy to go to meetings right now."

But when she asks the question, I notice a wrenching in my gut and I feel my anxiety level go up. I hear my voice getting louder and faster as I rattle off excuses.

But this time, I say to myself, "Wow, I'm defensive about something." Voila, an opening to deal with the real problem.

I sit down after the call and write down my thoughts, trying to figure out what I'm defensive about by doing a Backtrack. When it is completed, I am aware of what is making me feel defensive. I decide to call my sponsor back and discuss the whole problem even though I feel uncomfortable. End of conflict. Serious growth!

With some practice in recognizing defensive behavior, I can learn to interrupt myself right in the middle of the defensiveness.

For instance, I'm on the phone with the sponsor. I feel a wrench in my gut and realize I have an urge to exaggerate (a nice way to describe a lie). Rather than jump in and create a mess, I stop and say to myself, "Something is wrong here."

Then I make choices. I can choose to ask my sponsor if I may call her back in a few minutes. The pause gives me time to write and think about the situation before I talk.

Or, even better, I can tell her I have noticed an upsetting feeling and I'm not sure what's it about. Honesty, directness . . .what a concept!

Defensive Cue Words

I never . . .
I just . . .
I always . . .
I only . . .
Yes, but . . .

These words minimize and justify.
If something is a *fact,* it doesn't need to be justified or minimized.

Feeling the need to alter another's perception about events is called . . .

Denial

What compulsive behaviors surfaced?

A common result of the unsuccessful resolution of a problem is the appearance (or reappearance) of compulsive behaviors such as overworking, mind racing, overeating, anorexia-like behaviors, gambling, sexual acting out, overspending. Behaviors are labeled compulsive when they cause problems for you but you continue them anyway. Your compulsive behaviors then become the central focus of your life.

Locking into compulsive behaviors is sometimes a mechanism to avoid noticing deeper, more painful situations or feelings. One way to approach this struggle is to ask yourself, "What am I trying to avoid?" Then handle the issue immediately. Sometimes, direct action causes compulsive behaviors to disappear.

Take prompt and swift action if compulsive behaviors have appeared in your life. They are a major sign of trouble.

Which of the 12 steps can be most useful?

Applying one of the 12-steps of AA will be wonderfully helpful in every life situation. You will have an almost unbeatable combination when you use 12-step principles in combination with other effective problem solving techniques.

It is a commonly held philosophy in 12-step programs that the steps hold the answer to any problem. I agree. The difficulty for most people arises when they can't figure out how to apply the steps in a specific situation. This difficulty is more common than you imagine.

One question I ask of everyone who describes a problem to me in the course of their treatment is, "Which of the 12-steps can you use to help you in this situation?"

But, suppose you can't do abstract thinking yet.

Abstract thinking means you comprehend concepts and ideas. In contrast, concrete thinking means you only understand things you can see, touch, or smell.

Inherent in my 12-step question is a request for the person to think abstractly, but often in early recovery, they can't.

You say to them, "The answer is there!"

They nod in agreement, but say to themselves, "I knew I couldn't do this recovery thing. I don't even understand what she's asking me."

The solution lies in combining the use of one of the 12-steps with a problem solving technique. First apply the technique, then understanding the step will flow easily. For many people, it doesn't work the other way around.

People have been following this plan for years in the 12-step programs. Many times sponsors suggest techniques to help a sponsee learn to be more effective in applying one of the steps. For example, writing a journal or talking to others is suggested.

Problem solving techniques are not offered instead of a step, they are offered to augment the step.

If you didn't have this problem to distract you, what other problem would you have to notice and deal with?

The answer to this question often reveals the true, underlying problem. You have become good at setting up smoke screens to keep from noticing and resolving your underlying issues.

This is my personal mantra. Whenever I feel crazy as a loon, I ask myself the question. "What if I didn't have this problem to distract me? What other problem would I have to see and deal with?"

Then I answer my question with self-talk, "So work on the underlying problem and the current situation will dissolve."

Think of it this way, if I subconsciously *created* the current situation to keep from facing an underlying one, when I face it, the created situation will disappear.

Construct a Rational/Irrational Analysis.

Refer to the chart on page 167 to learn how to do a similar analysis. Write the Situation or Problem at the top of the page. Then draw a line down the middle. On the left side write rational (factual) thoughts, feelings, urges and actions. On the right side write Irrational (not factual), thoughts, feelings, urges and actions.

At first, you may try to put irrational thoughts on the rational side. It may be beneficial to ask your sponsor or recovery group to help you decide where to place your automatic thinking about the situation or problem at hand.

Work this analysis from top to the bottom. Once you have figured out where to place your automatic thought, brainstorm other ways to express the thought. In other words, if your thought is irrational, identify possible rational thoughts about the situation. Then complete the chart. Reflect, "If I'm thinking this thought, then I'm probably feeling this." And, "If I'm feeling this way, I'll probably have an urge to do this action, which will ultimately result in what behavior?"

Notice how eye opening it is to explore and then look at other options for automatic thoughts.

Rational/Irrational Analysis

Situation: Sponsor embarrassed me in front of group.

RATIONAL	IRRATIONAL
Thought: I bet she was having a bad day. Her behavior was probably not about me but I was embarrassed anyway.	**Thought:** I must be pretty worthless for her to talk to me like that in front of everyone.
Feelings: Disappointed, irritated.	**Feelings:** Shame, anger embarrassment,
Urges: Call her aside and tell her she hurt my feelings.	**Urges:** Run away and hide.
Action: Call her aside and assertively confront her.	**Action:** Pretend there is nothing wrong. Stay away from meetings and don't call sponsor. Avoid confrontation at all costs.

What are at least three options for handling this problem?

One of the main things that keeps you stuck in a problem is that you see no way out. You're cornered. You feel you are, "Damned if you do and damned if you don't."

For a moment, throw out that thinking. Don't consider the problem's outcome. Look at three or more possible options for handling the problem. You're missing something important if you are saying, "There is only one thing to do and I'm doing it."

You always have choices in life. The disease of addiction often blinds you to them but that does not mean the choices don't exist.

Go on a fact-finding mission. Accumulate information. It may help to pretend you are a friend or some other objective person outside yourself. What would they say are your options?

You may find it easier to arrive at the choices available by looking at a problem from an outside perspective. Talk to other persons. Ask them how they handle similar difficulties. You will soon begin to stack up potential options. Remember this is a fact-finding mission, now is not the time to judge options, only to accumulate them.

How many choices did you get? Were you surprised?

For each of these options, what is the worst, the best and the most likely result?

Here you are asked to do some rational thinking. Evaluate your options based on the information you have accumulated. Pretend the problem is a business deal that may or may not be interesting to you. Mentally stand back from the problem and evaluate it without passion, use only rational thinking. Base your evaluation of the options available to you on factual information, not on your feelings.

Have you prayed/meditated about this yet? If not, why?

It's amazing how people believe themselves to be spiritual beings, yet leave that power out of their everyday lives. It is not enough to pray for your already-decided-upon preferred outcome.

Pray, instead, for an open mind so that your heart is willing to look for a healthy answer. Follow up your prayers with the earthly foot-work necessary to solve the problem giving you a powerful one-two punch.

Imagine wanting to build a strong table. You have several pieces of wood and an electric skill saw. You have wood glue, sanders, varnish - all the necessary components. But it all just sits there until you plug that saw into the power source.

Until you first tap into the power source, you will not make a strong table. No power, no production.

Likewise, until you plug yourself into your "higher power" source, you will probably not solve your problems successfully.

You will solve this problem by . . .

You have examined the problem, looked at your options, considered the results, and plugged into a power source. It's time to decide and act. All the thinking in the world won't solve the problem. You have to act.

What if you are having problems with taking action? There is nothing wrong with getting assistance from others to help you get started. I often suggest looking for a "coach". We do it for sports, why not life?

Let the coach know what's going on. Relate the entire process you went through to solve the problem. Ask for encouragement to take the last step off the cliff. Sometimes, you can even ask the coach to jump with you.

When all else fails, act as if you *want* to take that last step. Even though you yearn to fight action, remind yourself you took lots of care to make the best possible choice. You can literally talk yourself into taking action.

What is the lesson you can learn from this experience?

As important as finding a solution to a problem is identifying the lesson to be learned by solving the problem. If it is true you have problems for a specific reason in the grand scheme of your life, then you need to go further than the solution.

You can expect the problem to repeat with equal or greater intensity if you have not learned an important life lesson along with finding a solution. This does not mean that if you figure out the lesson, there will be no repeat of the problem. However, if you internalize the life lesson, there will be no need to have that specific problem again.

Internalizing means you learn it from the inside out. Instead of the lesson being a coat you put on, it becomes the lining of your stomach walls. You will know it like you know your name, your fears, your parents. It exists within.

The acquiring of Universal Principles is the foundation necessary to solve your Life Problems. By all means, don't fail to acquire them. This is your opportunity to mend those holes in the Soul Wound. Go for it.

Spirit Vault

The third step of the 12-steps suggests that you, ". . . made a decision to turn your will and your life over to the care of God as you understood Him." This is certainly easier said than done. To help themselves, many people construct what is called a "God Box." I call it a "Spirit Vault".

Choose some type of container. You are going to deposit in it the problems over which you have no control. Write down the problem using the method described in this chapter. Answer all the questions as suggested.

Then fold up the paper, ask your higher power for the ability to deal with the problem according to His/Her or It's will. Place the paper into the Spirit Vault. More often than can be attributed to coincidence, an amazing thing happens. *The problem and its pain are eased.*

CHAPTER 12

CORE ISSUES

"A great many people think they are thinking when they are merely rearranging their prejudices." William James

Wrestling with a Core Issue is as if you are a student pilot in a plane. The crew dies and the ship is stuck on automatic pilot. You're afraid to take the controls of the plane off automatic pilot and try flying it yourself even though you know the plane will crash if you don't.

Core Issues are the central struggles of your life. They are the underpinnings of your behavior. They operate subconsciously. The lack of awareness surrounding the Core Issue may be in response to the intensity of the pain.

You may believe ignorance is bliss. However, if changing self-defeating behavior is your goal, ignorance is *not* bliss. Your Core Issues are a driving force in your journey through life.

What is a Core Issue?
A Core Issue is the result of a Soul Wound left unresolved. It is the automatic pilot of our life,

causing systematic, generally irrational reactions to everyday life situations.

FACTS ABOUT CORE ISSUES

How we get them.

Chapter 5 discussed Soul Wounds, the very painful, generally long-term problems which are often the result of trauma. Some examples of trauma include, but are not limited to: addiction, rape, physical or extreme verbal abuse, sexual abuse, incest, childhood neglect, abuse or abandonment. Soul Wounds grow into Core Issues when they are unresolved - when they fester.

Some people endure tragedies and traumas in their lives without developing a life-long self-destructive system. However, if traumas are not dealt with appropriately and completely at the time of occurrence, they create Core Issues. The trauma itself is not the problem. How it is managed creates the problem.

This is good news! It means that should traumas happen to you or your loved ones now or in the future, you can take immediate steps (discuss it, get help, don't hide it) to minimize the damage and prevent long-term ramifications.

However, you have to paddle your canoe where it is now. You are dealing with issues long past that are effecting your present and future.

Core Issues cause systematic, generally irrational reactions to life situations.

Core Issues are common.

Most adults have Core Issues. Unfortunately, the abuse and trauma responsible for them is common in the world. The impact of Core Issues on a person's life can be massive. Yet most people never explore, let alone resolve or manage their Core Issues.

Having worked on Core Issues does not mean you're finished.

This is a major myth, crippling progress. You may have the idea that if you worked on these issues, you're through with them.

You would be shocked to know the number of recovering people who are miserable. They sit for hours and hours in clinics explaining to a therapist why their Core Issue is not the problem now.

Just a hint here, if you feel a need to spend time explaining why something is, "not a problem", it may *be* the problem.

175

Defensiveness is one clear sign that a problem exists. Truth requires no long-winded explanation. A problem is factual or it ain't, period. All those hours spent throwing up defenses are wasted time.

I'm not saying here that every problem you have is caused by a Core Issue. (I wish it were that simple). People are much more complex than that. What is important for you to know is that Core Issues are *often* the source of difficulties in your life.

Core Issues DO NOT cause chemical dependency.

It is critical you don't put the cart before the horse if you want to deal successfully with your addiction. Many chemically dependent persons believe their trauma brought on their addiction. NOT SO!!

Chemical Dependency is a separate, primary disease in its own right. You would be addicted to chemicals whether or not you had traumas. There are mountains of clinical data proving this fact conclusively. Yet somehow the dangerous myth that past trauma causes addiction, persists.

It is vitally important for you to understand the relationship between your disease and your trauma. If you believe your trauma is the cause of addiction, you may harbor the secret idea that

176

when you resolve the trauma, you can drink or drug again. Though you may consciously deny you think this way, the facts often prove otherwise.

For example, think of people you know who decided it was their sexual abuse causing their addiction. They became so involved in working on their sexual abuse issues they "forgot" they were addicted and drank or used again. I can't tell you the number of times I've seen this sad pattern.

So what *is* the relationship between Core Issues and your addiction? Core Issues and the difficulties that come with them, can interfere with the recovery process. Core Issues get in your way so you have difficulty making healthy choices. Since the recovery process is a series of healthy choices, your Core Issues can be the origin of a dry relapse.

Core issues do not cause addiction but they can interfere with the recovery process

The Role of Core Issues in Dry Relapse.

For an example, you have a Soul Wound of childhood abandonment. This is common among recovering people. Assume you've been in big time denial about it. You have an Insufficient Resolution. You were badly hurt. You are still hurting but you don't acknowledge the Soul Wound's effect on your life.

Soul Wound + *Insufficient Resolution* = *Core Issue*

Because your Core Issue is so dreadfully painful, you develop Survival Skills to keep it from being "jostled." You believe if you can keep anyone from touching or bothering the wound, it will get better or cease to exist.

Once, when I had a broken foot it seemed to me as if everyone on earth was trying to step on it. I guarded it obsessively. I certainly wasn't going to let anyone step on it.

In much the same way, you protect a Core Issue. You build Survival Skills to prevent anyone from "touching" your Soul Wound.

What are Survival Skills people use? Some of them are defensiveness, dependency or counter dependency, developing commpulsive behaviors (gambling, or overworking are two), attempting to control people, places, and things, obsessive thoughts, focusing on other situations in your life and more.

Look at an example - the Core Issue of childhood abandonment. Persons with this issue frequently attempt to control other people - their Survival Skill. The result of trying to alleviate your pain by attempting to control others is a Diseased Belief System. You fill your head with automatic irrational beliefs, absolutely certain they are true.

Your unconscious self-talk may be statements such as, "If I am nice enough to others, they won't leave me." Or, "If I'm strong enough, others won't leave me."

Core Issue + Survival Skills
= Diseased Belief System

The result of your unconscious self-talk is a powerful irrational belief that if you are nice enough to others you can avoid devastating pain - like, "You won't step on my broken foot if I am nice to you." Right!

This belief overrides your common sense. Then you consistently behave as if this irrational idea is the truth. Even though you *tell* me you don't believe your irrational idea, your *actions* show you do believe it. You encounter hundreds, maybe thousands of situations in your life where you can superimpose this irrational idea.

Remember what I said in Chapter 8 about irrational thoughts? Basically, irrational thoughts lead to extreme feelings which lead to unhealthy urges and result in self-defeating actions.

An event happens. You tell yourself a lie about it. You convince yourself the lie is not a lie. You have intense feelings. Your resulting actions are not in your best interest. **Situations** lead to **Thoughts** which lead to **Feelings** which lead to **Urges** and then **Actions**.

Real life problems confront each of you on a regular basis. For those in recovery, small life problems handled with irrational beliefs can grow into giant monsters. Fostering irrational ideas, you can convince yourself you are perfectly right and others are surely wrong. You feel angry or hurt. You isolate. Depression becomes a factor. You build a case against the people in your life who will not support your irrational belief and against "that 12-step program."

More life problems crop up. You are so

stressed you can't handle them. Even problems you could manage easily last week are now a major issue. Other obsessive behaviors appear as you try to get a grip on your lack of control.

Down, down, down. Welcome to Dry Relapse.

Diseased Belief System

X Life Problems

=

the Beginning

of

Dry Relapse

Gathering "proof" your Self-Centered Belief System is accurate.

One of the most destructive side effects of this process is the need to prove your diseased Belief System is accurate. The irrational self-talk acting as a buffer for your Soul Wound commands you to behave in a self-destructive way.

To illustrate, look at Billie J's case. She has an unresolved Soul Wound of childhood sexual abuse. The abuse forms her Core Issue. As she grew, her intense pain persisted. Billie developed a Self-centered Belief System to manage it.

She began to believe she had done something to cause the abuse. Somehow she was responsible. She thought if she had been more alert, less sexy or a better person, this terrible thing would not have happened to her.

A set of survival skills emerged. She gained weight so she wouldn't be sexually attractive. She became hyper-vigilant, watching everything and everyone for signs of potential abuse. And she tried to be a "good girl."

These weren't just a few traits she possessed. Over time they became the central focus of her life. She firmly believed she had to act out these beliefs or else she would be abused again.

Billie's beliefs were subconscious, she was not aware of them but they were a heavy load for a young girl.

Billie entered her adult years and began dating. She continued to gather evidence that her beliefs were true. She was attracted to abusive men.

She would try to keep them from abusing her. She would gain more weight, watch them like a hawk to anticipate their needs and be a very, very good girl.

They would abuse her anyway. Eventually, she would leave the relationship, only to find another one just like it.

Meanwhile, her alcoholism was growing by leaps and bounds. Finally, she bottomed out and decided to go into a recovery program.

As long as she focused on nothing but recovery, she did well. Then she met a man and entered into a relationship. Guess what, he was an abusive guy!

Eight months of chaos and pain later, she decided recovery wasn't making her happy, she was worthless after all and wanted to kill herself.

Luckily, a friend intervened and helped her get treatment.

Billie tried to control her abuse by gathering "evidence" to support her irrational belief system. The hope that she could use her irrational belief system to govern the pain of her past abuse led her down a sorrowful path.

Billie is just one example of how this "proof" gathering works. Those with Self-Centered Belief Systems are always busy seeking proof their belief is true.

If you believe you will be abandoned if you don't leave others first, you will look for someone who will abandon you, thereby giving you the opportunity to leave them first. Then you can say, "See, I knew it!"

If you believe that if others really knew you, they wouldn't like you, then you find others who won't accept you as you are. When they don't accept you, you can point to their behavior and say, "See, I knew it!"

Effect of Core Issues on Recovery and Relapse.

Follow a specific case through this process for a clear idea of how it works.

Look at the illustration on page 190, *Effects of Core Issues on Recovery and Relapse* and follow the progress of John B.

John is 32. He is recovering from cocaine and alcohol addiction. He was in recovery for 18 months. He followed the 12-Step program, went to meetings, obtained a sponsor and worked the steps to the best of his ability.

Nevertheless, after 18 months of sobriety, one

day he found himself drunk and high and wondering, "What happened?"

John reported his relapse experience when he first began his Recovery Enhancement work.

John said, "I just don't understand. Everything was going great. The problem has to be my wife. I mean, I know nobody makes you get drunk and all, but we have constant problems. She gripes at me for everything. It was getting worse and worse. I should have left her a long time ago. So that's what I'm doing now. It's the only way I'll stay sober."

When John looked at his relapse he perceived he was doing fine. Then his wife nagged him and he had to get drunk. Yeah, sure.

He believes his version of his relapse to the bottom of his heart. It is his reality.

When he looked at the illustration on page 192, *Effects of Core Issue on Recovery and Relapse,* he was able to trace his climb up the Recovery Hill. He could relate to Life Problems/Situations and his slip down the Relapse Slide.

However, for John nothing in the "sky" part of the drawing existed. He could see no connection between a Self-Centered Belief System on his

186

part, or any survival skills and certainly none of that Core Issue stuff.

After completing his Recovery Enhancement work, John has a different point of view. He now describes his relapse like this . . .

"For about fourteen months, I was doing okay. I did the things I was supposed to do to stay sober and was starting to get some of the benefits, you know, the promises of the 12-step program.

I didn't realize it, but my wife was getting scared I would like my AA life so much I wouldn't need or want her anymore. It wasn't true, but that's what she thought. But instead of saying it right out, she started nagging me - sort of hoping to get my attention. That kind of thing.

"I also brought my own baggage into the problem. I have a bunch of unfinished business from my Dad's alcoholism and it left me with the idea that everybody would leave me sooner or later. I got such a fear of being abandoned by people, that the way I've always handled it - my survival way - was to leave them first.

Basically, instead of talking it out with my wife, I got defensive. The more defensive I got, the angrier she got and more certain she was losing me.

And the angrier she got, the more certain I

was that I was losing her. So my survival skill kicked in and I believed I had to push her away before she left me. What a crazy circle we were in. We were making our biggest fears come true.

"Eventually, the agony, all the fear - it got to be too much and I felt completely out of control. The only way I could figure out how to get back in control - even though I knew it was only temporary - was to drink and use again."

Refer again to that drawing on page 191. John's Soul Wound was his abandonment by his father. This painful event was never resolved sufficiently and therefore became a Core Issue.

As a child John developed a "Self-Centered Belief System" to support the idea that he was the cause of the problem. In other words, John believed his father abandoned him because John did or did not behave in a specific manner. In John's eyes, the abandonment was all his fault.

Subconsciously he concluded the world revolved around him and his issue: "I am the center of the universe, everything that happens is because or about me."

Consider this. If you believed to the core of your being that your parent left because of your actions, wouldn't that hurt terribly?

John developed Survival Skills to manage the

pain of abandonment and the subsequent Self-Centered Belief System. One Survival Skill he used was to leave others when he felt fearful they planned to abandon him.

Carrying all this baggage, John gets sober.

He would have his Core Issue whether or not he was an alcoholic, but the alcohol helped him mask his dysfunction.

In the drawing, when the "clouds" of Core Issues "rained" down their natural products of distorted beliefs and Survival Skills, John plunged down the Relapse Slide. It was a process. One event logically followed another.

He begins his Recovery Enhancement Program by climbing the Recovery Hill. After working through the critical matters of early sobriety, he is ready to work on his Core Issue.

Effects of Core Issue on Recovery and Relapse

SOUL WOUND +
INSUFFICIENT RESOLUTION

SOUL WOUND +
SUFFICIENT RESOLUTION

CORE ISSUE

Principle-
Centered
Belief
System

Self-
Centered
Belief
System

Healthy
Life
Skills

Survival
Skills

RECOVERY HILL

RELAPSE SLIDE

Life Problems/Situations

Irrational Thoughts

Extreme Feelings

Unhealthy Urges

Selt- Defeating Actions

Repeats S-T-F-U-A

Justify
Using / Drinking

Wet Relapse
or Mental
Breakdown

Identification of Core Issues.

There is no short cut through this work. You must *Trust the Process*. The exercises and text in this book are designed to help you accomplish the identification of your Core Issues. No one can do it for you. Others may see your Core Issue but that is irrelevant. You must understand the way your Core Issue effects your life before you will be able to work it through.

Identify your Core Issue by:
♦ Going through your life history.
♦ Telling your history to someone else.
♦ Understanding the nature of wet and dry relapse.
♦ Practicing rational thinking.
♦ Doing many Backtracks.
♦ Searching through your history, your thinking and your Backtracks for patterns of behavior.
♦ Defining the individual dominos in your relapse slide.

Once you identify your Core Issue, what can you do about it?

Develop a plan, that's what. There are no magic wands to manage your Core Issue. Hard work is necessary.

The good news is that once you have

completed the process of identifying the Core Issue fueling your dry relapses, you will know exactly where to focus your efforts.

Many people start their relapse therapy convinced of what causes their relapses. They are surprised, and eventually gratified, to find out differently.

Details of the following steps will be developed in Chapter Thirteen, Developing a Recovery Enhancement Plan

Approach this tangled web of dry relapse logically. Look at the process that created your difficulty.

First, you suffered the trauma that created the **Soul Wound**. Unfortunately, you cannot go back in time to change the situation that created your Soul Wound. The past is gone forever.

Your work in the present time is the identification and acknowledgment of the hurt. Ask someone with whom you feel safe to discuss your pain with you. Talking about your past trauma will help you manage the pain. The next step is to let your feelings flow as you write, write, write. Write about your feelings, past and present. Write letters to the people you feel have caused your pain. Just write! You may choose never to mail the letters but write them anyway.

The **second** step in the process is **Insufficient Resolution**. There are methods to help you heal old traumas. Much more about this subject later.

The **third** piece in this process is the **Core Issue**. You will work on gut level identification of your Core Issue. Management of Core Issues will be a result of your other work.

The **fourth** part is the **Self-Centered Belief System.** Think of methods you personally know (or have heard of from other people) used to help conquer Self-Centered Beliefs. Talk to people who have the humility that accompanies a lack of self-centeredness. Ask them how they achieved their ability to be objective.

You are not trying to become "other-centered" in this exercise. That's as dysfunctional as being self-centered. Make it your goal to become "higher power-centered," leading to a growth in spirituality, principles and values.

Fifth is **Survival Skills**. This is where the concept of trusting the process really impacts. You will have major difficulties letting go of Survival Skills until you work through the first four steps on this list.

Mastering each step makes it easier to do the next one. Without logical progression people tend to get stuck and often give up. The strength comes in the process. Rely on it.

Working on Survival Skills is difficult, period. However, after you have taken the first four steps listed above, you can apply a powerful technique, "fake it until you make it."

The technique involves adjusting your self-talk and behaving in a new way even though you feel pulled to act the way you "always" have. Go ahead and feel all the feelings, then have a rational chat with yourself to find a healthier approach. Then, act on that strategy.

Just because you feel impelled to act a certain way doesn't mean you *must* behave that way. However, until you have done the preparatory work you can tell yourself rational self-talk ad infinitum. The addictive side of your personality will shout it down. You will revert to giving your old Survival Skills control of your behaviour.

Conclusion

Dealing with Core Issues is difficult. It is, however, a fantasy to think that by ignoring them they will somehow magically heal or they will simply stop bothering you. In truth, unresolved Core Issues "bother" you every single day, often without your conscious knowledge.

Remember the crew on the aircraft you've been riding in since the first page of this chapter? They died a very long time ago. You've been on automatic pilot for most of your life. Now is your chance to invest in a process that will enable you take the controls of the plane in hand and learn to fly the craft yourself. It *is* frightening but it's also exhilarating and challenging.

You can master the ability to fly toward a powerful, spiritual life style.

CHAPTER 13

FAMILIES OF THE HEART

"Emotional Bank Accounts create commerce between hearts. Regular deposits of commitments made and kept result in rising levels of trust."
Stephen Covey

Thus far, your focus has been on internal work. That was no accident. A great deal of personal work must precede relationship work. Concentrate on healing yourself first. *Trust the Process*.

You may have attempted healing your relationships first and found that approach does not work. Frustration was your reward. Often, you only managed to reinforce the Irrational Thoughts keeping you unhappy and dysfunctional.

Now that you have completed the work from the first eleven chapters to the best of your ability, it is time to acquire a **Family of the Heart**.

What is a Family of the Heart (FOTH)?

A Family of the Heart is a carefully selected, mutually beneficial group of safe friends who provide opportunities for you to grow beyond your Core Issues.

The original term, "Family of the Heart" was the brain-child of Kathy Bortko, a Certified Relapse Prevention Specialist. Kathy, a dedicated professional, is a big part of my personal FOTH. Her courage to face each day despite the painful, crippling disease she battles, is a lesson of its own.

Why do we need a Family of the Heart?
You will acrue many positive benefits from your group. Your FOTH offers support during a difficult time in your life. You gain an opportunity for personal growth that may not be present under other circumstances.

Many people use their 12-step group for support and growth.

Some people develop a FOTH without ever giving it a name or even realizing what they have. They just notice they are improving, getting happier, more able to forgive and release their "character defects." These are some of the benefits of having a Family of the Heart.

There are three primary purposes for having a FOTH. The first is support. Second is the acquiring and internalizing of critical Universal Principles. The third is the disproving of Irrational Thoughts. All these are mechanisms for healing *beyond* your Core Issues.

How can you benefit from a FOTH?

You know a number of your patterns, issues and Survival Skills at this point in the process of Recovery Enhancement You know the Relapse Dominos of your dry relapse process. You've figured out the problem. What you need now is the solution to the problem.

What you originally thought was your problem turned out to be only a symptom. As you realized while doing your Recovery Enhancement work, you need to be open to new ways of thinking in order to find the true source of your difficulty. The healing process also requires you to use strategies different from those you've been using up to now.

Turn to your FOTH to help you disprove your Irrational Thoughts. Your group can help you learn the principles needed to provide sufficient resolution or management of your Soul Wound.

Irrational thoughts are found in statements beginning with, "I must", "I can't", "I should", or "I always".

In the past, you set your Irrational Thoughts in stone. You spent years gathering evidence to support them and to disprove the need for principles such as, honesty and spirituality.

Your need to "prove" your Irrational Thoughts drove you to set up situations to make your irrational thoughts seem true. For example, you unconsciously selected friends and significant others who would leave you if you became angry.

You tried everything to prevent feeling or showing anger. But most people have angry feelings at times. Anger is a legitimate human emotion. When you do not recognize, express, or own your anger, it builds. Eventually, you have a mountain of anger that will not stay suppressed. It will be released!

The presented anger may show up as cutting sarcasm, criticism, depression or else you explode into violence. Then others *will* leave you. You are behaving in ways that are vicious or even dangerous to them.

A FOTH will help to find your missing principles and disprove your irrational ideas, such as, "I can never be angry or they'll leave me."

199

Missing Principles and accompanying Irrational Thoughts are different for every individual. Only you can determine yours.

You will not know what needs attention until you complete the earlier work. Within the exercises is the information you need to know about your specific missing Principles and accompanying Irrational Thoughts.

How do you work with a FOTH?

Practice, practice, practice.

You spent years setting up ways to *prove* your Irrational Thoughts to yourself, now you must reverse the process and *disprove* them.

Here is an example of how you can dispute the Irrational Thought, "I can never be angry or they'll leave me."

Choose a FOTH member to help you. First, interview the person and discuss what you are trying to accomplish. You *prearrange* to express your anger and agree you will not leave each other's friendship. It is important for the both of you to agree to ground rules such as, "No violence ever."

In the interview process, in addition to your Irrational Thoughts, you also discuss your FOTH partner's Irrational Thoughts that may be causing problems in their life. You agree to work on both of your issues.

Spend some time with your FOTH partner developing a positive bond. Allow sufficient time to build a trust level.

As your friendship progresses, begin your work by appropriately expressing anger about minor events. Test your own and your partner's response. As you start to feel safer, begin expressing your feelings about issues closer and closer to you. At the same time, your FOTH partner is also working on disproving their own bothersome Irrational Thoughts.

Eventually, you will want to express an angry feeling about an act of your FOTH partner. You will probably have some difficult feelings about confrontation but with the help of your partner, you can process those feelings. Your FOTH member knows it is vital that they listen to you without leaving you. When they don't leave, you begin to internalize the idea it's possible to be honest with others.

You will find many opportunities in your innovative relationship to make progress both on acquiring Universal Principles and disproving Irrational Thoughts.

Progression from Soul Wound to Wet Relapse

1. A **Soul Wound** occurs. (Father abandoned you as a child.)

2. It has **Insufficient Resolution**. (Principles needed to manage the problem were not acquired and internalized.)

3. The lack of resolution created your **Core Issue.** (Abandonment.)

4. To protect the **Core Issue** in your subconscious mind, a **Self-Centered Belief System** was developed. ("This is all my fault, Father left me because I got angry.")

5. This diseased **Self-Centered Belief System** was supported by an **Irrational Thought**. ("I can't get angry or you will leave me.")

6. To further insulate from pain, **Survival Skills** emerged. (Denial of anger at all costs.)

7. You are compelled to deny and suppress your anger. Since most people feel some anger nearly every day, the anger builds and builds in the form of **Life Problems** often expressed as sarcasm. The problems cause constant pain. **(Dry Relapse.)**

8. Your anger explodes or you take the only pathway you see - drinking or drugging until you don't feel the anger or the pain. **(Wet Relapse.)**

202

Search beyond the flaws

The work of a FOTH inherently includes the acquiring of the principle of Brotherly Love which begins with the acceptance of flaws in others. It's been said the flaws we "can't stand" in others are a reflection of our own intolerable defects.

Have you ever had a "type" of person with a particularly annoying personality trait seem to follow you around? Everywhere you turn, someone with that irritating attribute pops up. Look for important information in the experience. You may be being given a powerful opportunity to grow. Perhaps this is an opportunity to become aware of a Universal Principle you are lacking.

One goal while working with your FOTH will be to search beyond the flaws of family members. Find the significance for you in your search, then extract the valuable lesson you've been unable to benefit from in the past.

Life-altering ideas are to be found in Dr. Stephen Covey's bestseller *Seven Habits of Highly Effective People*. Dr. Covey says, "Seek first to understand, then to be understood." This is one of the most powerful concepts I've heard in a long time.

The idea is, you can empathize with others and get to know them well by finding out what they are searching for. Don't try to find out for an underlying greedy purpose, do it because it's right. Take the time.

You may complain that nobody understands you. When was the last time you made a sincere effort to understand someone else? How can you expect appreciation yourself if you don't extend it to others? Try to understand other people. Don't wait for them to offer understanding first. Then, miraculously, people will want to know you and to help you. They will also respect you.

Wholeness is the bottom line of Recovery Enhancement. Dr. Covey's book is about the completion of self and your relationship with the world. The book is sometimes found in the Management section of bookstores but it is about becoming a whole person. Do yourself a favor and read this book.

Dangers of FOTH.

Recovering people have set up Families of the Heart for years, though they never used this name for it. You set it up it unconsciously and with no thought, direction or purpose other than friendship or romance. You found yourself in relationships with people you "liked."

The problem is that many of you are attempting to complete the internal struggles that started in your family of origin. Without understanding or knowing your underlying reasons, you select individuals for your group to fill the role of a family member with whom you have unfinished business.

Then, you subconsciouly recreate situations to provide opportunities for you to "do it right." so you can magically straighten out those earlier situations.

Unfortunately, past situations usually can't be resolved without major conscious work leading to changing of thought patterns, feelings and behaviors. Relationships established to help you meet your needs dissolve into dysfunction. You need or demand from others what they are incapable of giving you. In other words, you set up codependent relationships.

You can easily create dysfunctional, codependent relationships if you do not complete the work of the earlier chapters of this book before you attempt to work on your Family of the Heart. You will lack a clear direction and understanding of the underlying Core Issues, missing Universal Principles, Irrational Thoughts and Survival Skills.

How can you possibly develop a system to correct a problem if you don't know what skills you need? You may create more pain than you had before you began.

Who are good candidates for your FOTH?

Consider several qualities when selecting participants in your FOTH. A desirable quality in a FOTH candidate is a mind open to trying new approaches to problems.

Some people select FOTH members from their own recovery program. Others utilize anyone in the "recovery process" whether their addiction is people, pills, food or substances. An essential criteria is that the candidate be growing or willing to grow.

I suggest you steer clear of a romantic involvement. It is much too easy to get swept away in the passion of the relationship and forget the purpose. Begin with FOTH members of the same sex. Perhaps, after you have had some success with a same sex FOTH, you will be prepared to grow with the opposite sex.

How do you get this Family?

For the first time in your life, you get to pick your family! Begin with a diligent, logical search. After completing your work from the earlier chapters, you know what Core Issue, Universal Principle and Irrational Thought to correct.

Select persons you believe exhibit the characteristics you need to complete your work. Interview each person.

An exercise in the workbook describes this interview process.

Take time to do a *personal* inventory before you begin the selection process. Know what you want from them. Know what support you have to offer them in return. Suggest your candidates read this book before they agree to participate in this work with you. Above all, be honest and up front about the process and your goals. Resolve to be invariably candid with your FOTH about your thoughts and feelings.

My Family of the Heart story.
Jerry forever changed my life. I wish I could say that I purposely choose Jerry as a member of my FOTH but, at the time, the idea hadn't been conceived.

Jerry was, and is, my husband's best friend. He has been abstinent 17 years. When I first became sober, I saw him as angry, judgmental and frightening, just like my father. He wasn't drinking but he wasn't happy, joyous and free, either. In short, he was someone to avoid at all costs.

God had other plans. Jerry and his wife, Eileen, became our constant companions. We bought adjoining lake lots. Our families began to spend whole weekends together.

As my program developed, I began to take time to listen to Jerry. I slowly began to recognize the beauty within him . . . a beauty he does not recognize.

Our relationship grew as I began to silently affirm his inner value. My view of him changed. First he was a frightening man, then a puzzle and finally became a true friend to whom I would trust my life.

You may think, "Wow, that Jerry has surely changed." No, he's still the same guy he always was. The person who changed was me. I changed my attitude and gradually he seemed different to me. He says the same kinds of things but they don't sound the same to me. Now, I perceive what he relates as funny and witty. I feel comfortable being his friend.

This is not the end of the story. The miracle came as a completely unexpected by-product of my different perception of Jerry.

Over time, I began to notice that the actions and words of my Dad were just like Jerry's. I could see the same feelings hidden under Jerry's irascible comments were my Dad's feelings. My heart began to thaw. My entire view of my Dad changed. The anger and pain dissipated. I found forgiveness, understanding and love.

My father's words and actions were the same

as always. What changed was the way I heard them.

My Core Issues were powerlessness and low self-esteem. I acquired the Principle of Brotherly love - other words for acceptance. I disproved my Irrational Thoughts, "I must make others happy" and "I must be perfect."

Thank you, Jerry.

Have you figured out the Secret Goal?

CHAPTER 14

DRY RELAPSE INTERVENTION

"You have to leave the city of your comfort and go into the wilderness of your intuition. What you'll discover will be wonderful. What you'll discover is yourself."   Alan Alda

Dry relapse is a process always preceding wet relapse. If you understand dry relapse you will have the powerful ability to stop the awful slide into wet relapse. Develop effective techniques to stop a dry relapse and you will never need to worry about a wet one.

At this point, you have examined your past, practiced writing Backtracks, looked for patterns of behavior and recognized many of your Relapse Dominos. It's time to turn knowledge into action.

Part 1: Complete the front of your Dry Relapse Domino Cards

Tim Sullivan, MSW and a student in the CENAPS school for Certification for Relapse Prevention Specialists developed the following art therapy technique.

I'll never forget the lesson I learned from Tim. We were on a bus to the Chicago airport. I felt tired and drained. I wanted to sit alone and relax. Tim was excited about the workshop we had attended. Bubbling with enthusiasm, he began to tell me about a method he uses for relapse prevention. Indeed, the information was important and his excitement contagious.

Continue the process you started with your Domino Cards in Chapter 10, *Naming Dry Relapse Dominos.*

You recall that each Domino described a specific increment of your personal Relapse Slide. The Dominos were extracted from your Backtracks and placed in chronological order.

Take out your pile of Domino Cards now and read them out loud. Include the Thoughts, Feelings, Urges and Actions (T-F-U-A's). Focus on each Domino. Connect with each of them. Do they tell your Dry Relapse story?

Start the next step in this process by making a drawing to represent each Relapse Domino. Place your drawings on the bottom of the front side of every card. The name of the Domino and it's T-F-U-A's will be on the top half of the card.

You will be using the backs of the cards for a later exercise so don't use them now.

One of Jane's Dry Relapse Dominos is, "I work late and frantically." The irrational thought accompanying this idea is, "I must work like a dog or they'll fire me." This idea is a reflection of Jane's addiction voice.

On the top half of the front of the Dry Relapse Domino card you have the name, the irrational idea and the Thoughts, Feelings, Urges and Action written. On the bottom half of the front side you've got a drawing representing working late and frantically. Your drawing should try to capture the fear and stress and the urge to run away while trying harder and harder.

No way!

I know you're thinking, "I'm not an artist. I can't do this." I promise that doesn't matter. This exercise is not an art contest.

The reason for using a picture is the old adage, "A picture is worth a thousand words." It is true. Studies show many people learn better from picture representations than from words alone because a picture stays in your mind longer. You will be able to recognize your Dry Relapse Slide faster when you use both words and pictures.

Early identification and intervention using effective techniques to prevent or stop the Dry Relapse process is your goal. The more tools you have enabling faster interruption of the Dry Relapse Slide, the better off you are.

People using this drawing exercise find it works well once they get over their shyness about sketching. Draw in pencil. Then if you *can't stand* your attempt, you can erase it. Deal?

Dry Relapse Dominos

Adding the Art

Part 2: Complete the Back of the Dry Relapse Dominos

You have completed the front of the Dominos, now it's time to finish the back side.

Refer to the *Rational/Irrational Analysis* on page 168. This drawing shows both the irrational thought behind most of our problems and its flip side, the rational thought.

There is always a rational answer or backtalk when you have an irrational thought. Some people think of it as their "addiction voice" or their "recovery voice." I call it Rational Backtalk. Focus on these thoughts to feel more reasonable and rational. Your stress will go down and solutions often appear. To help you focus, on the back of each Domino Card write the Rational Backtalk for each situation on the front of the card. The statements will be your recovery voice disputing your distorted thinking.

Take the irrational idea, "I must work like a dog or they'll fire me," and write a Rational Backtalk. For example, "Overworking will not help. When I'm frazzled I make more mistakes and am less efficient." Write more than one Rational Backtalk for each idea so you have alternative methods of managing the situation.

Lastly, on the bottom card back, write a list of coping methods to use if this Domino falls.

Your Goals

are within your grasp.

Don't stop now.

Complete your work.

Watch the miracle

happen to you.

Part 3: Watch for Falling Dominos Chart

The next item of business in this intervention process is to complete the "Watch for Falling Dominos" chart. This chart helps you check the status of your personal Dry Relapse Dominos.

In Chapter 10, you named your Dry Relapse Dominos, a series of thoughts, feelings or actions that appear when you're sliding into dysfunction. The Dominos depict repeating patterns.

Once you decide on a final list of Dominos, plug it into the form, *Watch for Falling Relapse Dominos.* Check your list daily. You will be surprised at the progress you make toward eliminating Relapse Dominos from your life style.

Many patterns will change just because of the awareness created when you make checking your list a part of your daily routine. Other patterns will be slower to respond and require more attention.

However, keep track of the frequency these slower-to-respond Dominos occur. You will empower yourself to correct your own course long before you need to have others intervene. It's amazing!

It isn't "bad" to have Dominos fall. Don't beat yourself up for it. It is normal to make mistakes. The time you spend berating yourself over misteps is a total waste of time and energy.

Instead, focus on the positive aspect. Yes,

today you noticed a Dry Relapse Domino fell, but a few months ago you would not have even known it was part of your pattern. Now, you have a process to use for problem solving. You have tools to interrupt problem habits.

You may have frequently falling Dominos for a while. That's okay. Comfort yourself with the knowledge that you are not worse than you were before, its just that now you're aware of your patterns . . . the first step for change.

You decide how you want to use the information you glean from this exercise. One approach I recommend is an agreement you make with yourself. If you check off a predecided number of Dominos, then you must complete a Backtrack for the two days before that increase in falling Relapse Dominos began.

One thing is for certain, it is not enough to just check the list. You must take action to correct the problems. Fortunately, I have found that people who are aware something is going wrong and are still early in a dry relapse process are quite anxious to take action to correct it.

I share your experiences as a recovering person and know a big problem happens when we are well into a dry relapse before we notice. By then, we are in a nose dive. Normal problem solving efforts often don't work.

Watch for Falling Dominos

If more than **3** Dominos fall in a single day or **20** in a week, I will do a Backtrack and review my intervention plan.

Week of **3/18 - 3/24/96** Total # Dominos that fell in week **20** Name of Relapse Dominos	Mon 3/18	Tues 3/19	Wed 3/20	Thur 3/21	Fri 3/22	Sat 3/23	Sun 3/24	Wkly totals for each Domino
1. I compare myself to others and decide I'm no good.						✓		2
2. I pretend it doesn't matter I think I don't measure up.			✓					1
3. I feel defeated, powerless and angy.					✓			1
4. I can't stop thinking about work.			✓		✓	✓		2
5. I work late and frantically.	✓							1
6. I have an urge to run away.			✓					1
7. I'm tired and skip a badly needed meeting.								0
8. I have an urge to relapse into smoking.								0
9. I eat ice cream at bedtime, ignore spouse.								0
10. I sleep badly, get up late.					✓			1
11. I skip breakfast, drink extra coffee, go to work.					✓			1
12. I feel hurt when others go to lunch without me.	✓				✓			2
13. I feel paranoid, rageful and vindictive.						✓		1
14. I relapse with cigarettes, skip lunch						✓		1
15. I can't focus on work, memory shot, thinking fuzzy.					✓	✓	✓	3
16. I eat a candy bar in the afternoon.		✓				✓		2
17. I blow up at spouse and believe it is his fault.				✓	✓			1
Total number of Dominos that fell each day	2	3	3	1	7	4	1	20

219

Watch for Falling Dominos

If more than _____ Dominos fall in a day or _____ in a week, I will do a Backtrack and review my intervention plan.

Week of _____
Total # Dominos that fell in the week _____

Name of Relapse Dominos	Mon	Tues	Wed	Thur	Fri	Sat	Sun	Wkly totals for each Domino
1.								
2.								
3.								
4.								
5.								
6.								
7.								
8.								
9.								
10.								
11.								
12.								
13.								
14.								
15.								
16.								
17.								
Total number of Dominos that fell each day								

Part 4: Dry Relapse Process Intervention Plan

Utilize both your own efforts and the efforts of others near you to develop a solid plan to take you out of dry relapse. Your plan should help you to return to Recovery Hill quickly. The sooner you can get back on track, the less pain you will inflict on yourself and others.

In case your self-intervention methods fail, you need to have an intervention network and a clear plan developed and available. The purpose of your plan will be to interrupt the relapse process as early as possible, long before the use of alcohol and/or drugs causes devastating consequences. Hopefully, even before the dry relapse has caused a great deal of pain.

It is critical for you to understand the relapse process, including its domino effect. You will need to have a list of your own relapse dominos to be able to complete your plan.

The Intervention Plan has three parts:

1. Select people in your recovery network to assist you in this intervention.
2. Tell them the signs of dry relapse to watch for in your behavior.
3. Tell them exactly what they must do to help you get out of your dry relapse cycle.

Why you need an Intervention Plan?

An incredible 60-70% of those who attempt recovery for the first time have a Wet Relapse. Many authorities consider this to be an optimistic figure. An Intervention Plan can lessen the chance you will downslide into the use of chemicals.

Spouses and other loved ones often see Dry Relapse behaviors occurring before you are aware of them. They know you are in trouble long before you do, but they don't know how to help. Give your recovery network permission in advance to intervene. Discuss with them the behaviors to look for. Give them clear instruction about the best ways to help you. While awareness of your problem behaviors may be unsettling to your spouse, your friends and your FOTH, a plan is also comforting. They will know what to do to help.

To whom do you give your Intervention Plan?

Your Family of the Heart and others exposed to your behavior on a regular basis (i.e., spouse, sponsor, close sibling, or co-worker you trust) are the best people to enlist for help. Limit those involved in your plan. Three to five people is good.

"Warning signs of trouble" you should use.

Write Relapse Dominos in behavioral terms. For instance, one of your Backtracks reveals a pattern of angry behavior when you're in a Dry Relapse. Rather than calling the Relapse Domino "anger" write *what you do* when you're angry (i.e., slam doors, throw things, call others names, clam up).

Make the "warning signs of trouble" very concrete, never vague. Since you are asking others to watch for these signs, the more specific you are, the better results you'll have. Always ask yourself if the other person has enough information to know when you are displaying warning signs.

Don't overlook involving your spouse in this process. Hopefully they are working an Alanon program. If so, each of you complete an Intervention Plan. Alanoners also have relapses. Their old destructive behavior is witnessed by others and can also be intervened upon. Ideally, each of you will develop an Intervention Plan. Read it to each other aloud at home or in your Recovery Enhancement group.

What actions can my support network take?

The "Actions I want you to take" section of the Intervention Plan (see page 226) shows a progression of responses. At first, the Actions are mild, gentle proddings to alert you to the fact that you have some falling Relapse Dominos.

For example, the first action might be to show you your Intervention Plan and tell you they love you and are worried about you. If the dry relapse process doesn't stop after the gentle reminders, then the Significant Other must be willing to take more drastic action.

Their next possible action might be calling your sponsor. They may discuss with your sponsor what behaviors they see and their fears about what is happening.

When you write your Intervention Plan, make sure the actions you ask of your support group are:

- Actions they can take.
- The desired acts are concrete and clear behaviors.
- The actions will get your attention without making you so upset you can't possibly respond, (i.e., Don't tell them to shout at you when you know that won't work).

Actions that have been helpful to others include having a support network person call the others in your group. Then assemble them all together to talk to you, (be sure to include their name and phone number when you write the Plan).

A more intense action to consider, set up an intervention with your EAP or therapist and the family.

Your Plan must be concrete, easy to understand and execute. It must be carefully thought out with progressively stronger interventions designed to urge you back onto your Recovery Hill. Be creative but realistic. You can do it.

Present the Plan to your intervention network

You have decided who you want to have in your network, prepared the "Dry Relapse Intervention Plan", and made a copy for each person. Now is the time to sit down with them and explain the concept. I suggest you select a comfortable, quiet setting. Write an explanation in advance so you are clear about what you want to say. It is highly likely that no one in your selected group has participated in a plan like this before now.

You want to empower others to help you, but keep in mind, these people are doing you a favor. Be sure to approach them with that thought in mind.

Dry Relapse Intervention Plan

Date_____

Dear_____

     Since chemical dependency is a disease into which I may relapse, it is wise for me to consider an intervention plan. Relapse is a process, not an event. It is a domino effect. Therefore, I will show many warning signs of trouble before I actually use alcohol/drugs. I am constructing this plan while I am sober and rational. My plan is to stop the problem in dry relapse. Please don't be fooled by my denial. If I am in relapse, I will make many false statements and deny the problem . . . my disease will be active again. Please be assured these are the actions I want you to take. **The plan below is the course that may save my life.**

Signature_____

My signs of trouble (Relapse Dominos) predicting a relapse is impending may look like this.

Dry Relapse Domino #1

Dry Relapse Domino #2

Dry Relapse Domino #3

If I am actively drinking/using again, I will exhibit these behaviors:

Actions I want you to take:

Action #1

If problem continues, Action #2

If problem continues, Action #3

If problem continues, Action #4

If all else fails, please

CHAPTER 15

DEVELOPING A RECOVERY ENHANCEMENT PLAN

"If you are distressed by anything external, the pain is not due to the thing itself, but to your estimate of it; and this you have the power to revoke at any moment."
Marcus Aurelius 121 - 180 A.D.

The Recovery Enhancement Plan is a personalized plan designed to systematically improve, enrich and widen your recovery experience. What you have tasted thus far is more relief than recovery. You worked at removing the impediments of progress holding you back. Your unresolved Core Issues, the lack of certain Universal Principles and Irrational Thoughts have prevented you from realizing your potential.

Typically, we in recovery have been grandiose (another survival skill) or we've been without hope or vision for our future. The gray behavior area in the middle of these black or white expanses has escaped us. We may have had the impression that the gray area was our enemy. Think again. It's time to examine where to go from here.

Leave behind your preconceived notions of your fate and your destination in life. Step outside the constraints holding you down and prepare to look at yourself hard and long.

Imagine yourself free of your self-imposed limitations. You are in a space ship looking down at the earth. From this perspective anything is possible.

Mission Statement

A Mission Statement is a written description of your purposes and directions in life. In it, you examine what is important to you. This may be a difficult project but I promise you can do it.

Your Mission Statement will be your guide in determining your direction. It will help you to decide whether or not what you are currently doing is in your best interest. It can also help you decide whether or not a proposed project is in keeping with your mission. Your Mission Statement has incredible power to guide you in making healthy decisions and to reduce or even eliminate some forms of guilt.

Creating a Mission Statement was my impetus for writing this book. I wasn't even considering writing it. In fact, I was moving in a different direction altogether. However, once I constructed my Mission Statement, I realized helping others in the healing process is a primary concern for me. It became clear to me that this book would be in keeping with my mission.

All my excuses and rationalizations about why I couldn't possibly write the book disappeared. I knew in my heart this was exactly what I was supposed to do. No more questions. No more hesitation. I was able to decide easily. My direction has been clear ever since I wrote my Mission Statement. I refer to it every day. It now hangs on the wall in my office near my computer.

In *Seven Habits of Highly Effective People*, Dr. Covey suggests that in order to construct a Mission Statement, consider how you would like to be remembered when you are dead. Things that are insignificant as well as those that really matter will be obvious when thought of in this way.

For example, I am dead and about to be laid to rest. As my husband approaches the front of the church preparing to say a few words to our family and friends, how do I want him to remember me? As a hard worker or a perfect housekeeper? Probably not. I am more interested in his thinking about how deeply I loved him, how important our love was to me, how passionately I felt about helping others and about growing in personal recovery work.

How do I want my children to remember me?

As someone they could count on to set them straight about any subject they happened to mention, or as a loving, generous, non-judgmental mom?

How do I want my colleagues and patients to remember me? As someone who knew how to make money or head a committee? Or do I want to be remembered as someone who thirsted to learn more, give more, help more.

Think about the kinds of activities you find most fulfilling. What types of behaviors or areas of endeavor give you a sense of completeness? Perhaps you are most happy when you're working with young people, seeing them grow and blossom. Yet, you claim you don't have time for the activity that gives you the most fulfillment in life.

What if you were to recognize this work as your mission? See how a Mission Statement could identify your truly important life goals then empower you to make them happen?

Make a list of the activities that gave you the greatest satisfaction in your life. On your list could be anything from making your child smile to making the very best brick on the market. The most important thing about the action is that it must feel fulfilling to YOU.

Create your Mission Statement by answering

all the questions in the above paragraphs for yourself. Take the time and care to concentrate your answers in the construction of your mission statement. Read it every day.

My personal mission is to love my husband, family and friends deeply, to passionately help in the healing process, to leave judging in the hands of God, to grow spiritually, and to learn every day.

A Mission Statement isn't just noble sounding words or a goal for which to strive. It is a reflection of a deeply held conviction. You can't write the words and then believe in them. Use a soul-searching process to reveal what is of primary importance toYOU and what is not.

The beauty of using a Mission Statement as a life guide is that you can easily see if a new project is in keeping with what you really want in your life. People often lose track of what's important when dealing with their every day routine. Your Mission Statement helps you stay centered.

You must find your direction from inside, write it down on paper and follow it in order to move from the relief stage to the recovery stage. A clear Mission Statement will release you from the fears and anxieties that come from not knowing if this project or that move is right.

The time and energy formerly spent fretting, trying to decide what action is best, can now be effectively put to use. You can accomplish what really matters to you. Day to day living is simpler and, at the same time, more meaningful. Self-esteem, confidence and spirituality expand. Relief turns into Recovery!

You are standing at the edge of a miracle

Goal Setting

Now that you have a working concept of your life direction, it is time to set goals. Start with an understanding of how a goal is related to a mission. To reiterate, a Mission Statement is a written description of your purposes and directions in life. The *mission* is to find your true heading on your personal compass. Your compass consistently points you in *your* right direction.

Goals are the targets you want to hit along the way. Using travel as an analogy, let's say my internal compass (Mission Statement) points me in the direction of north. I head north from Houston (where I am now). While I'm traveling north I cross nothing but open prairie (no specific target or goal). This is not rewarding, but I am in line with my compass and mission. Or, I decide to travel to Dallas, then Oklahoma City, then Chicago (goals I set).

When I make it to each of these cities, I feel a sense of accomplishment and a boost to my self-esteem because I reached a small goal I set for myself. More significantly, I feel an increased confidence as I continue my trip. When my energy ebbs between Oklahoma City and Chicago, I persevere by reminding myself of the goals I have achieved. My ability to stick it out is strikingly increased with my positive self-talk.

This "trip" illustrates the relationship of the Mission Statement to Goal Setting. Both have critical and separate functions.

So how do you decide on Goals?

First of all, you can't set accurate goals until you have defined your mission. How will you know which direction is right for you if you don't have a compass (Mission Statement) to find your personal North? You may find your way to lovely goals but in the absolutely wrong direction for you. What a waste of your time and energy.

Along with most humans, I have had the experience of accomplishing many things in my life that didn't have anything to do with my life mission. These accomplishments had value but they didn't move me toward the fulfillment of my Mission.

Once you have constructed your Mission Statement and know which direction is right for you, then begin your goals work.

Goals are the logical outgrowth of the Mission Statement. In other words, if you know which way is north on your personal compass, then you can figure out the destinations along the way.

For example, if my mission is to be the best parent possible, there are some logical goals along that path. One goal may be to learn more skills in parenting. Another goal may be to spend more time with my child, setting aside an hour or half-hour every day for the child one-on-one. Do you see how goals help you with your mission?

Long Term Goals

The next step to consider is, where do you want to be in the long range, maybe five years from now? Here's your chance to think big!

Consider the different areas of your Mission Statement. Using my Mission Statement as an example, I have encompassed several roles, wife, mother and friend. I also incorporated my personal growth work, both professional and spiritual.

Look at your long term goals. Consider your roles and personal growth, then choose how you want to accomplish each of your goals. Using your Mission Statement as the lodestar, what are your targets for each role and each personal growth area?

Most of all, dream your dreams. When others tell you you aren't able to do what you plan, do not assume they are correct. Did you know Stephen King received hundreds of rejection slips from publishers before his first novel was accepted?

You have a right to your dreams. If you can't imagine succeeding, it is not likely to happen.

Maybe you don't allow yourself to dream because you're afraid you may fail. Guess what? You probably will fail sometimes. But with persistence, you will succeed sometimes, too. Edison tried 2,000 times to light up the light bulb before it worked. That means he "failed" 1,999 times. No one disagrees that his one "success" made up for all the "failures."

Even though you fear failure, I encourage you to push past your fear and try, try, try. The only failure is failing to try. I also suggest you take the word "failure" out of your vocabulary. Use other descriptive words such as, "error" or "learning opportunity."

Resistance to long range planning

Some people believe the 12-step concept of "One day at a time" means they should not consider long term plans. It appears to be almost a superstition that by planning where they would like to be in the future, they jinx their program.

Don't believe it, this is a myth. Setting goals and missions lead you in a spiritually sound direction. This process does not preclude living today to the fullest. Instead, by knowing you are moving in a spiritually sound direction, you will have more energy to live one day at a time.

You can fully enjoy the sounds of the birds and the smells of the forests. You will have a sense of well being coming from being centered and realizing that nothing is wrong today.

Some people believe having long term goals locks them into those goals. The are afraid they must be rigid and controlling in order to accomplish them. Another myth.

When you have target goals backed by a Mission Statement embodying your principles, you are spiritually centered. In consequence, when a problem appears, threatening one of your goals, you have the tools to resolve the issue logically. If necessary and in keeping with your mission, you can even change or modify your goals. That's up to you. You are the one in charge of changing your course if necessary.

Still others believe that setting long term goals is a waste of their time. This is the biggest myth of all. Nothing saves time as much as having a clear direction. The amount of time you spend dancing around trying to figure out "what is the right thing to do?" can be much more effectively used having fun or truly BEING WITH your family.

Short Term Goals

Once you buy the idea of long term goals, it is logical and important to set up short term goals. The best way to get to a long range target goal is to set small goals along the way.

For instance, I want to be an excellent pianist in five years. How can I do it? First of all I make a series of consecutive short term goals. The first one is obtaining a piano; second, beginning lessons; third, setting up and staying with a practicing schedule; fourth, giving my first recital; fifth, finishing the beginner book; sixth, finishing the first grade book. You get the idea. No one can become an excellent pianist without completing the short term goals.

Suppose you only focused on the long range goal of being an excellent pianist. You would tire of the attempt soon because it is taking such a long time.

However, if you set all the little goals along the way, then you will feel a sense of accomplishment each time one is completed. You can see your progress toward your long range goal. The result is your confidence, self-esteem and commitment go up.

Plan your short term goals in succession. For instance, you set a long term goal for next year. Next, you need to plan a series of small goals that will result in the completion of your yearly goal.

My long term goal for next year is to have 100,000 copies of this book in the hands of people who can benefit from it. To accomplish my goal, there are specific actions I must do this week, next week, next month, and in six months.

My goal for this week is to finish writing this chapter. For next week, my goal is to finish the final chapter. Next month, I will do my final review. In three months, I will review the galleys. In six months, the books will arrive in the mail and the promotion tour will begin. See the logical progression? I can't start a promotion tour until I complete this chapter! My short term goals are a direct reflection of my long term goal.

Feeding your Spiritual Growth

Thus far, I have discussed writing a Mission Statement and Setting Goals, two aspects of the Recovery Enhancement Plan. When you have completed the work on these two, you are ready to move into the next area of the plan - Spiritual Growth.

At this point, you are standing at the edge of the miracle. It is very close. When you have come this far, spiritual growth is practically inevitable. Still, you need to structure the opportunities to continue your development. There are literally hundreds of activities you can pursue to enhance your Spiritual Growth. On the following two pages is a chart showing a few of them to get you started.

Also on the chart are a few of the negative actions that can interfere with your Spiritual Growth.

Spiritual Feeding

List of Do's	Description
Read positive literature	Seven Habits of Highly Effective People, Daily Meditations, classic literature, biographies such as Anwar Sadat and Winston Churchill.
Encourage others	Offer *sincere* words of praise to others for their deeds, ideas and spirit. Focus on the good in others.
Help others	Once you have filled your own basket of spirituality, use some energy to give help to others. Teach others a skill you have or take dinner to a sick friend.
Learn new skills	Learn how to do woodworking or gardening or how to use that blasted computer.
Follow artistic pursuits	Play the piano, paint, write *The Great American Novel*
Read Scriptures	Very fulfilling for those who participate in this form of spiritual growth.
Write in a journal daily	Highly recommended. Your writings are for you only. A terrific growth tool.
Become involved with a well grounded group of spiritual people.	This can range from a Sunday School group to a group organized to work on the Recovery Enhancement Workbook.
Have fun	Play games, see a funny movie. Find reasons to laugh. Nothing heals like laughter.
Prepare and follow a Relapse Prevention Plan	Your personal Relapse Intervention Plan gives you the foundation to pursue continued spiritual growth.

240

Obstacles to Spiritual Feeding

List of Don'ts	Descriptions
Watch negative TV shows	Whatever you feed, grows. If you fill your mind with murder, mayhem and violence then that is what grows.
Participate in gossip	Gossip is negative. When you gossip, even though you believe you have love in what you say, you are damaging your soul.
Judging others	You don't have the right to decide what is wrong or right for others. Choose your actions for yourself and acknowledge others right to do the same. In judging others, you place yourself above them, an easy place from which to fall.
Use drugs or alcohol	Nothing kills spirituality as surely as introducing mind altering chemicals into your body .

Whatever you feed grows. If you feed your spirit negative thoughts and energy, then negative thoughts and energy grow. Feed your spirit positive energy to make that strength grow.

You have made significant progress, but it is important to understand that you are constantly moving in one direction or another. If you are not moving forward, you are sliding backward. Maintain your progress, or better yet, continue to move ahead. Feed your spirit.

The Faith Builder

This "spiritual feeding" idea is all well and good but some of you need hard evidence before you entrust so much to a "higher power." In that case, accumulate data to find the evidence. Sounds very scientific doesn't it?

Almost everyday (no less than 3 times a week) people experience small, positive coincidences. They are incidents you may overlook or feel are your just due to make up for all the other garbage in your life. Look again! These small, positive coincidences are very important parts of a bigger picture.

Now, begin to gather evidence. Obtain a spiral notebook or, if you choose, one of those fancy bound books with blank pages. On the front of the notebook write "Positive Coincidences" and the beginning date. Begin entering your coincidences in this log. I have yet to find anyone who has less than three of these a week. Many people find at least one surprising, positive coincidence per day.

What kind of coincidences? Well, for instance, you're at a meeting and you hear the EXACT thing you need to hear right then. Or an insurance reimbursement check arrives in your mail box when you need money desperately. Or you are feeling blue and an old friend calls you.

These positive coincidences begin to mount up. When you look at them all together in your notebook, they become a powerful faith builder. It is impossible to look at all your "coincidences" and not realize there is a strong, positive force active in your life. Voila! You gain faith.

When you feel sad and believe you've been forgotten by your higher power or that there isn't one after all, take out your log. Prove to yourself your higher power is alive and well. Your log of positive coincidences quickly becomes a Miracle Log of evidence gathered directly from your life experiences.

Try this exercise. You'll be inspired by its power.

Whatever you feed grows.

If you feed your **Recovery**, it grows.

If you feed your **disease,** it grows.

You choose every day.

DISEASE

RECOVERY

CHAPTER 16

CONCLUSION

"They say that time changes things, but you actually have to change them yourself."
Andy Warhol

Are you ready for a tee shirt that says, "I Survived the Recovery Enhancement Process?"

You have worked hard, challenged old ideas, looked for and found patterns of dysfunction, worked to change them, formed new bonds with a Family of the Heart, added new life principles, set up systems to protect your recovery and started to feed your spirit. Whew, that's impressive!

In 1988 when I first met Terry Gorski, a visionary and pioneer in the field of Relapse Prevention, I knew his theories had great power. I went through his certification process for Relapse Prevention Specialist. In the training, the therapists become the clients. They practice the application of Terry's theories with each other.

I have not been the same person since that experience. I can't adequately express my gratitude for all the ways Terry Gorski's ideas and training help me.

I had a pervasive sense of helplessness before completing my personal relapse prevention work. If you had asked me if I believed myself helpless,

I would have denied it. But deep-down I believed the important things needing to be done were the responsiblity of others. I believed I was a victim of circumstances, my childhood script. I was convinced my destiny was to stay in it.

It wasn't as if I hadn't tried to change my script. I had tried therapy, chemical dependency treatment, twelve steps, religion, you name it, I tried it. All the work combined had never fully exposed my learned helplessness. I certainly never felt the empowerment I have after completing my Recovery Enhancement work.

Until then, I was bedeviled and paralyzed by the ordinary occurences of life. If a light bulb was burned out, I didn't change it. I just complained. To be totally honest, back then it didn't even occur to me to change it.

Now, instead of complaining about things that used to keep me stuck, I methodically change them. If people I know are negative and nonsupportive, I find a new circle of friends. If others ask me to do something I don't want to do, I refuse. What freedom!

When I came to this place in my recovery, my heart was full. I wanted to share what I have with others in a way that will have meaning for them. My desire to help and share was the beginning of my mission to help relapse prone people (wet and dry). I feel a driving force within, a strong reason to get up in the morning, to read every shred I can find written on the subject, and to give of myself and my knowledge at every opportunity.

In my past, I had experienced moments of excitement about one idea or another. I wondered if this was another whim that would fade away. It wasn't. Before, I had never had the willingness to stick with it. Eight years later, I am sure of this accomplishment as a reality. After I finished my personal Recovery Enhancement work, the mission was no longer an effort. Actually, I don't know how I could have stopped it. It was a bit like a runaway train.

The wonder of this change can happen to you. Once you eliminate the blocks on your spirit and begin real spiritual growth, the future is incredibly bright. Now is the time to begin your wonderful journey. This is a power place for you to be.

Remember your Mission Statement? The impediments have been removed and your spiritual blocks exposed. You have a plan in place to manage or eliminate them. Literally any mission you select, any mission that fits your inner self, you can successfully follow.

Share your new knowledge with others in recovery. Help them to receive the gift of fulfilling recovery. Some people with whom I have worked choose to go slowly in this and others rush in with both feet. Some people organize a new Recovery Enhancement group and lead others into the process, watching them grow to new heights in their recovery. The way you choose as right for you is the one to take.

Picture this. You are relaxing by a cool, blue Caribbean lagoon. You have been holding a pebble in your hand. You toss the pebble into the water and watch it land. Then you see the ripples begin. One by one, in wider and wider circles until the single pebble has changed the entire water surface. Change begets change. One pebble, one person *can* make a difference. Trust the Process.

Trusting the process doesn't end here. Your growth has just begun. You will be a partner in watching it multiply ten fold, then ten fold again.

Goals of *Trust the Process*

In the first chapter my goals for this book were listed. You be the judge now. Were they accomplished? The goals were:

1. Explain the Recovery Enhancement Plan.
2. Motivate you to action.
3. Have fun.
4. Accomplish the Secret Goal.

Oh yes, I promised to reveal the secret goal. It is a primary one for me. I want this book to change your life in a positive, loving and permanent way. Did it happen?

> Today you cannot possibly
> imagine how you will
> grow, succeed and multiply
> in joy
> in the next five years

The end.

Bibliography

Alcoholics Anonymous. New York: Alcohol Anonymous World Services, Inc., 1955

Bell, Tammy L. *Preventing Adolescent Relapses.* Independence, MO: Herald House/ Independence Press, 1990

Brown, Stephanie. *Treating the Alcoholic: A Developmental Model of Recovery.* New York, NY: John Wiley & Sons, 1985..

Covey, Stephen R. *The Seven Habits of Highly Effective People.* New York, N.Y.: Simon & Schuster; Fireside Edition, 1990.

Daley, Dennis C. *Relapse: Conceptual, Research and Clinical Perspectives.* New York: The Haworth Press, 1988.

Gorski, Terence T. *Passages Through Recovery.* New York: A Harper-Hazeldon Book, The Hazeldon Foundation, 1989.

Gorski, Terence T. and Merlene Miller. *Staying Sober: A Guide for Relapse Prevention.* Independence, MO: Herald House/Independence Press, 1986

Jellinek, E.M. *The Disease Concept of Alcoholism.* New Haven, CT: College and University Press in association with Hillhouse Press (New Brunswick, NJ), 1960.

Marlatt, G.A. and Judith R. Gordon (eds.) *Relapse Prevention: Maintenance Strategies in the Treatment of Addictive Behaviors*. New York: The Guilford Press, 1985.

Miller, Merlene, Terence T. Gorski and David Miller. *Learning to Live Again*. Independence, MO: Herald House/Independence Press, 1986.

Ohlms, David, M.D. "The Disease of Alcoholism" film. Cahokia, IL: GWC, Inc., 1989

Trotter, Caryl. *Double Bind*. Independence, MO: Herald House/Independence Press, 1992

Twelve Steps and Twelve Traditions. New York: Alcoholics Anonymous Publishing, Inc.(now known as AA World Services, Inc.), 1957

Frequently Called Numbers

Addiction Relapse Prevention . . . . (713)469-9606

CENAPS Corporation . . . . (708)799-5000

GWC, Inc. (Ohlm's film) . . . . (800)851-5406

Herald House/Independence Press . (800)767-8181

Newjoy Press . . . . (800)876-1373

Index

254

Order Form

Please send me the following:

Amount	Item	Unit cost	Total
	Trust the Process Book	$15.95	
	Trust the Process Workbook	$15.95	

Postage & Handling		
1 book $1.40 1 workbook $1.40 1 workbook and book $1.90 Each additional book or workbook add .40 cents Orders of 10 or more books/workbooks will be invoiced separately.	Subtotal	
	*Tax	
	P&H	
	TOTAL	

California residents pay 7.25% sales tax

To place your order

Mail this coupon with your check for the total amount. Your order will be processed within 72 hours.

Please print clearly

Name_____

Address_____

City, State, Zip_____

Send your order to:

Newjoy Press, P.O. Box 3437, Ventura, CA 93006

Unconditional Guarantee
If, for any reason, you are not satisfied with your purchase,
return it and your money will be refunded.

Thank you for your order

Order Form

Please send me the following:

Amount	Item	Unit cost	Total
	Trust the Process Book	$15.95	
	Trust the Process Workbook	$15.95	
Postage & Handling 1 book $1.40 1 workbook $1.40 1 workbook and book $1.90 Each additional book or workbook add .40 cents Orders of 10 or more books/workbooks will be invoiced separately.		Subtotal	
		*Tax	
		P&H	
		TOTAL	

*California residents pay 7.25% sales tax

To place your order

Mail this coupon with your check for the total amount. Your order will be processed within 72 hours.

Please print clearly

Name_____

Address_____

City, State, Zip_____

Send your order to:

Newjoy Press, P.O. Box 3437, Ventura, CA 93006

Unconditional Guarantee
If, for any reason, you are not satisfied with your purchase,
return it and your money will be refunded.

Thank you for your order